ASTROLOGY AND NUMEROLOGY

Discover all the Secrets of the Universe by Knowing Horoscope & Zodiac Signs, Tarot, Enneagram, Kundalini Rising, & Empath Healing for Self-Discovery with Self-Esteem

CONTENTS

INTRODUCTION

Astrology Is a classic material, wrapped in myths and conjectures now, since whatever has been understood concerning that science has become oblivion through the years. But people still feel zodiac signs are interesting and may even have pleasure in hearing regarding their horoscopes more out of fun than whatever else. The signs have a lot to say about the person. While the exact characteristics and individual traits can only be predicted after a comprehensive study of the person's birth chart, the generic faculties common to this person's zodiac sign might be understood by studying the habits or nature of the particular individual. It is worth knowing individuals are segregated on the grounds of zodiac signs.

Zodiac Hints and people's characteristics

- Aries - An extremely confrontational voice, very competitive, mutually independent, adventuresome, freedom loving, bold, enthused, athletic, ambitious, reckless, dynamic, powerful, more confident, loud, warlike, dull, spontaneous, hard led, hasty, tenacious, hot flashes, strong willed, selfish, rude, enterprising, impulsive, achiever, risk taker, and unstoppable.

- Taurus - Preference for nice things, could be extremely materialistic, love better things in life, sometimes slow in reacting, great at currency management, likes outside, favors outdoor tasks such as gardening and farming, very practical down to earth, quite good desire, discriminated towards building, abhors changes.

- Gemini - A very great arguer, witty, flirtatious, trickster, adaptive, lively but can be offensive, inconsistent, and could be touchy, intellectual, easily pleased, quick witted, chatty, sociable butterfly, changeable, knowledge seeking, loves reading and writing, likes mental games, great good at multi-tasking.

- Cancer - Overly sensitive and painful, erratic mood alterations, romantic, sweet, nice, caring, nurturing, homey, motherly, favors home cooked meals, likes quality family time, environmentally conservative, withdrawal by the spectacle if feeling hurt or offended.

- Leo - Loving, loves kids, sensitive, enjoys jewelry and lavish, bold and stunning, bigger-than-life attitude, highly demanding, hard, prefers to become the middle of attention, smug, bright, conceited, pompous, strong-willed, loud, intelligent, loyal, higher vitality, very attractive, a distinguishing mane of thick hair.

- Virgo - Perfectionist, detail oriented, practical, critical, weatherproof, intellectual, intelligent, sharp witted, good communicating power, shrewd, emotional dexterity, penetrating, opinionated, judgmental, naturally bashful, helpful, organized, favors simplicity, enjoys things to take order and tidy, the way to justify things in a debate.

- Libra - Indecisive, frivolous, flirtatious, diplomatic, graceful, enjoys beauty and attractive objects, affirms equality and justice, social butterfly, pleasant manners, lazy, gracious, considerate, beautiful, idealistic, peace maker, a terrific judge.

- Scorpio - Secretive, positive, passionate, loyal, hypersensitive, athletic, mysterious, investigative, straining, powerful, resourceful, sensual, covetous, hot tempered, commanding, strong willed, magnetic, resilient, and excellent endurance, resourceful, revengeful.

- Sagittarius - Adventurous, friendly, individual, broad minded, enthused, brave, exceedingly optimistic, witty, intelligent, rebellious, freedom seeking, restrictions, flirtatious, natural entertainer, talkative, exaggerating, impulsive, dull, over-indulgent, a risk taker, owns childlike wonder, thirst for knowledge, philanthropic, deep, philosophical,

- Capricorn - Stubborn, stingy, argumentative, older, and reserved personality, cold or detached, attentive, hard worker, generous, likes responsibility, overly ambitious, self-oriented, teasing, status searching, respects power, career oriented, high endurance, and patience.

- Aquarius - Likes to help others, democratic, broad minded, reformer, deep, social equality, humanitarian, freedom oriented, trendy, cold or indifferent, bizarre, rebellious, inconsistent, unpredictable, original, highly opinionated, unique, sharp-tongued, friendly, idealistic, resolute, ingenious.

- Pisces - Dry, harmonious, friendly, creative, delightful smile and eyes, escapist, moody, lazy, affectionate, offensive.

Certain People still rely on astrology and believe in what their horoscope can signify about their own future. Although the present-day science neglects to comprehend astrology because a reliable discipline of science, many individuals still believe in astrology out of these faiths.

CHAPTER ONE

ASTROLOGY AND ZODIAC SIGNS

In Western astrology, astrological signs will be the twelve 30° sectors of the ecliptic, starting at the vernal equinox (one of those intersections of the ecliptic with the celestial equator), also called the First Point of Aries. The purchase price of the astrological indications is Aries, Taurus, Gemini, Cancer, Leo, Virgo, Libra, Scorpio, Sagittarius, Capricorn, Aquarius, and Pisces. Each business is known for a constellation it passes through.

The Concept of this zodiac started in Aztec astrology and was later influenced by Hellenistic culture. In accordance with astrology, celestial happenings relate to individual activity to the principle of "as above, so below", so the signs are held to be a symbol of feature modes of saying. Modern discoveries regarding the true nature of celestial objects have undermined the theoretical foundation for assigning significance to astrological signs, along with empirical scientific evaluation has shown that predictions and tips according to these systems are not accurate. Astrology is usually regarded as pseudo-science.

Various Approaches to measuring and dividing the sky are currently employed by differing strategies of astrology, although the heritage of the Zodiac's names and symbols stay persistent. Western astrology steps from Equinox and Solstice factors (points about equivalent, shortest and longest days of the tropical year), while Jyotisar or Vedic astrology steps across the equatorial plane (sidereal year). Precession contributes to Western astrology's zodiacal divisions not equivalent at the present era into the constellations that take similar names, while Jyotisar measurements still correspond with all the background constellations.

Western zodiac signals

While Western astrology is basically something of Greco roman culture, [citation needed] several its more basic concepts originated in Babylon. Isolated references to celestial "signs" in Sumerian sources are not sufficient to speak of a Sumerian zodiac. Specifically, the branch of the ecliptic in a dozen equal industries is a conceptual construction.

By The 4th century BC, Babylonian astronomy and its system of celestial omens influenced the culture of early Greece, as did the astrology of ancient Egypt by late 2 Nd century BC. That led, unlike the Mesopotamian convention, in a strong concentrate on the birth graph of the individual and in the creation of Horoscopic Potter, using the usage of this Ascendant (the rising level of the ecliptic, at the right time of birth), also of twelve houses. Association of the signs with Empedocles' four-dimensional elements was another major development from the characterization of their twelve signs.

The Body of astrological comprehension by the second century AD is described in Ptolemy's Tetrapylons, a work which has been to blame for astrology's successful disperse across Europe and the Middle East, also remained a benchmark for nearly seventeen centuries since later traditions made few substantial alterations to its core teachings.

The Next table enumerates the twelve divisions of celestial longitude, with all the Latin names (still popular) and the English translation (shine). Even the longitude intervals, being a mathematical branch, are shut to the very first endpoint (a) and open for the next (b) -- as an example, 30° of longitude could be the initial point of Taurus, not section of Aries. Association of calendar dates with astrological signs just makes sense if referring to Sun sign astrology.

Polarity as well as the four components

Empedocles, A fifth century BC Greek philosopher, identified Fire, Earth, Air, and Water as elements. He explained the nature of the world as an interaction between two conflicting principles predicted love and strife manipulating the 4 elements, and said why these 4 elements were virtually equal, of exactly the exact era, that all rules its province, and each possesses a unique individual character. Different mixtures of the

6

elements produced different natures of stuff. Empedocles said that those have been born together with near equal proportions of the four elements are more intelligent and have the most precise senses.

Each Sign is connected with a number of the classical elements, and such may be grouped based on polarity: Air and Fire signs are deemed positive or extrovert, masculine signs; whereas Water and Earth signs are considered unwanted or introvert, womanly signs. The four astrological elements can also be considered as an immediate equal to Hippocrates' personality types (sanguine = air; choleric = fire; melancholic = earth; phlegmatic = water). A modern approach discusses elements as "the energy stuff of experience" and the next table tries to outline their description through key words.

Aquarius - January 21 - February 19 Pisces - February 20- March 20 Aries - March 21 - April 20 Taurus - April 21 - May 2 1 Gemini - May 22 - June 21 Cancer - June 22 - July 22 Leo - July 23 -August 21 Virgo - August 22 - September 2-3 Libra - September 24 - October 23 Scorpio - October 24 - November 22 Sagittarius - November 23 - December 22 Capricorn - December 23 - January 20

Astrology Aries March 21 - April 19

Strength Keywords:

- Independent - Generous - Optimistic - Enthusiastic - Courageous

Weakness Key words:

- Moody - Short-tempered - Self Involved - Impulsive - Impatient

Mobility:

Aries Personalities are all independent. Being the first of the zodiac signs, they venture out and are go-getters, often resulting in the way in which. Their positive and magnetic personality often entices others to follow their thoughts due to their personalities bring excitement into the others' lives.

Friendship:

They are Superior friends they always keep an eye out for their friends with caring and generosity and can protect them if the demand arises and encourage them with their natural optimism. If confronted, they can turn to become quite childish and will fight with their aggressive nature and are known to have temper tantrums should they not receive their way.

Business:

Aries are activists. If a small business idea comes their way, they tend to plunge right in. More than willing to have a gamble and follow their own dreams and aims. But if success is not immediate, they tend to eliminate interest and quit readily. They are notorious for not finishing what they will have begun. That is because of the exceptionally low tolerance for boredom and lack of patience. When the excitement is finished out of their enterprise idea, they go off and hunt for it everywhere.

Temperament:

Independence Is crucial, they do not like to take orders from others and revel in getting their way. They can get childish or moody should they be given orders that they do not like and easily take offense to comments made. Aries are self-involved and will be timid, if they do not focus on the feelings of many others, can very quickly become spoiled and resented by others. To receive their way, they are going to tell a lie if it appears advantageous to act. They are however, not so great liars and other people can usually see them through.

Deep Interior:

Underneath The powerful, independent surface can lie insecurity. This is because of the intense drive to succeed and so they put too much pressure on their own, thus leading to self-doubt but the pure optimism and enthusiasm overtakes the underlying insecurity may never be known to others.

In A Nutshell:

Aries Is the initial of this zodiac signs which is the sign of their self. People born under this sign strongly project their personalities onto the others and can be quite self-oriented. Aries often venture outside into the entire world and leave opinions on the others that they are exciting, vibrant, and talkative. They tend to call home adventuresome lifestyles and want to be the center of attention, but rightly so as they are natural, optimistic leaders. Excited in their goals and enjoy the thrill of the hunt, "desiring is always better then becoming" is a good way to sum it up. Very impulsive and ordinarily do not think before they act - or speak. Too often Aries will say whatever pops in their thoughts and usually end up regretting it later!

Love, Sex and Relationships

What It is wanting to date an Aries Woman:

Dating Never lacks excitement. She is hot-blooded, and strong; therefore, you had better be ready to deal with the heat! The Aries woman is for whoever likes a different self-driven woman who can fend for himself and is not clingy and needy. She requires freedom. On her, the best portion of this relationship could be that the start, then your flicker is there, and she is attempting to grab you to be mesmerized. She will see happiness at a long-term relationship because she enjoys sharing everything with her or her partner. She will not only have a romantic partner but also a companion too. She includes an excellent need for passion and love, but she will not ever let a man behave as the master, so she believes her partner to become equal and so are not for domineering men. She will be loyal however she expects the exact same in return. She can be jealous because she wants a man to offer her all his attention, "all or nothing", therefore her jealously is rooted within her possessiveness she must be number 1 in his eyes. She will consistently encourage and give strength to her partner so that an Aries woman is great to have in times of despair or need, she will always be there for you. To get this happy ending, she wants to feel appreciated and loved.

What It is want up to now an Aries Person:

An Aries man has a lust for experience, if you are considering having a relationship be equipped for fast paced experience, novelty, and enthusiasm. He is always eager to try new things - including relationships. That is not to imply that every Aries man is only going to supply a thrilling and short-lived relationship, but this is normally the situation. He might stick around if you are the type of woman that enjoys with the person simply take the lead and basking in his glory. He loves challenge therefore if you are the girl to give obstacles to him like playing hard to get - he would stick around longer. Bear in mind, this guy is all about the thrill of the chase. Do not however, act as in case you never care for him. He needs you to be "swept off your feet" by him. Appear innocent- hard-to-get plus he is going to be wrapped round your little finger. Never make the most of his short temper will turn into a fury of anger and the manner leave and never return.

How to Attract:

Let Them know that you admire them, they flourish of followers and admiration. Let them know that you simply love their zest for life and which you just find them fascinating, they love praise more than other astrology hints. Compliment them emotionally and mentally, they like talk about intellectual issues and engage them in an energetic discussion, or even perhaps a friendly debate. They adore the battle and the stimulation of good, clever dialogue. Ask them for advice, make them know that you just look up in their mind. Remember, Aries is the first sign of the zodiac and the many forward and independent, they love followers. You should not be a push, usually do not keep your opinions to yourself because they are going to quickly get bored if you accept everything they say. Do not attempt to restrain them yet, they do not enjoy taking orders. Aries are extremely competent people therefore if you go together with their aims, you are certain to have a good time! If they have a suggestion for something to do, then go with the stream, they want to be in control of exactly what goes on.

Erogenous Zone:

The Mind is the powerful erogenous zone. Stroking their hair and rubbing their own scalp can make them feel relaxed and enhance their sensations. Nibble the ear, such as especially those men, they will not be able to resist this, he will acquire uncontrollable urges and you will shortly be all his!

Sex:

Straightforward, Aggressive, and daring and this can be reflected in their way to sex. Expect it to become both physical, rough, and quick, they prefer to control and have the upper position.

Taurus Astrology April 20 - May 20

Strength Keywords:

- Dependable - Continuous - Loyal - Patient - Generous

Weakness Keywords:

- Stubborn - Laziness - Possessive - Materialistic - Self-indulging

Independence:

Taurus Is perhaps not usually the one who ventures out in the unknown and leads the way, they are those which will stick to the pioneer and fortify and build upon the discovered, in other words they would be one who will "dot the I's and cross the T". This perseverance is given to them by their stubborn streak. This stubborn streak is the thing that gives their liberty. They like to do things in their way. They are perfectly fine on being alone, in this way things do how they want them to be carried out. Taurus is not a follower; however, they are not the brave one and so are totally independent. With their own friendships, they get things done and can do very well on their own.

Friendship:

A Taurus is a wonderful friend. They have couple close friends instead of many acquaintances. The couple people that they hold dear to them are guarded and protected. Their friends are treated like family and they are fiercely loyal and dependable. Taurus loves to be the hostess or host. Although perhaps not a complete social butterfly, they can be shy around strangers, but the individuals they let in their own lives are catered into if Taurus decides to throw a celebration, they decorate and exhibit everything. They are going to consistently gratify their close set of friends.

Business:

Taurus Is a strong businessperson. They have been the individuals who have massive perseverance, even when others have given them up, they rage on. They have a knack for fund and their financial advice is precious. They know where money is to be produced and can control and establish the path for their own success. Taurus are not frivolous spenders nevertheless they like to reside and surround themselves with nice possessions and food, which all adds up resulting in large spending customs. They will not devote their cash and induce their business to fail since they do, their security and equilibrium is going to be eliminated and this will result in them great stress.

Temperament:

Taurus Are intensely sensitive and painful, the smallest comment or damaging opinion is going to be obtained and they can easily get offended or hurt. Their stubborn streak results in laziness. They can be quite idle whenever someone gives them orders or wants them to act, they do not want to do. They Aren't idle as it pertains to themselves, even

Deep Indoors:

Taurus Are not keen on shift. Will be change is imminent, they become very apprehensive and worried. They usually do not like anything fresh because anything new is unknown and fear that the unknown. They need order in their own lives and when they do not have order, they get very anxious. Taurus will cut off from the unknown to be able to prevent the feelings of insecurity which arise when fresh experiences and situations are found. They do not express their feelings openly and their inner self is included and secretive. Many do not understand how sensitive Taurus they are hide it well. Because of this, they have been usually emotionally hurt when the wrong things are said, they simply take things too personally sometimes. They avoid discussing their emotions and many individuals never really know how they feel.

In A Nutshell:

Taurus May be the one that has immense dedication, even when others have given up, they anger on. Solid and constant, exactly enjoy the bull, which is Taurus' ideal symbol. They've a well-known reputation for being stubborn, that is not necessarily a terrible thing. The stubborn streak may make them butt heads and battle along with other strong personality types. Not keen on change, they enjoy the comfortable and regular comfort of life. Taurus is laid back rather than anyone to pick a fight but if some poor souls attempt to provoke, the anger is going to be understood, for they have a temper underneath the surface. They are extremely receptive to their own surroundings. They like decorations, color, and whatever appeals to all the senses. They like possessions and the Taurus home is nicely decorated with a great deal of things. Down to earth, they usually do not like gaudy, flashy or extraordinary things. They prefer comfortable and creative preferences and objects. Liking security, in every aspect of their lives out of home, to love, to career. They are sometimes secretive, opinionated, stingy, tend to be self-indulgent, lazy, and therefore are master procrastinators of the astrology zodiac! They do however have a strong, persistent drive which comes to life when they chose, no one would ever know they are idle. The key to that is that their laziness is pushed aside when it comes to themselves.

Love, Sex and Relationships

What It is like currently a Taurus Woman:

Taurus Women are experts in the art of attraction. She'll get what she wants but her patience is incredible, she will await that which she wants She needs stability and security and won't endure a man who is not straight with her and leads her along with uncertainty in long term. She's the conservative type, the sort of woman who is linked to the drive-in soft drink shop days of the 60's. She is down to the earth, protective, supportive, loving, devoted and loyal. She is openly affectionate in a relationship. Excellent for the man who likes to be nurtured and pampered, providing you are loyal and devoted. She is got too much to offer but she takes a lot in exchange. Remember, she is overly sensitive, but she might not seem so on the outside. Court her and always attempt to impress her and you will win her soul and she will be yours. Cross her, along with her temper will flare, she will turn out to be extremely stubborn. If you ever break her trust, it will be nearly impossible to achieve it back again.

What It is like up to now a Taurus Man:

The Taurus man is very sensible, he is not the guy to sweep you off your toes. He is sensible and down to ground. He wants a high-quality woman, perhaps not a woman for a single night. He will questionnaire carefully until he makes his approach. He is quite patient when it comes to a relationship. He will survey the problem and be sure the woman has something to supply him, before he supplies himself. He is a romantic man, he will place his woman on a base, protect her and cherish her. Once he is chosen his woman, he will be very generous, loyal, loyal. He is not a boring man; however, he is not for the girl who wants pleasure and adventure. He is for that woman who desires stability and relaxation, he is an extraordinary provider and is just an exceptionally fine choice for someone for the right woman. He is in this for the long term therefore commitment is not a problem with this man.

How to Attract:

Do Maybe not attempt to rush into a relationship. They are quite patient and expect you to be so overly. Make them laugh, even if they have been entertained and entertained with you, they will enjoy being together with you personally. The way to a Taurus' heart is through his or her heirs. Cook for them or offer to take them to some nice upscale restaurant. They like speaking about finance, company, money, and material possessions.

Erogenous Zone:

The Neck and throat are the popular spots. Gently rub the throat, kiss it lightly, lick at it gently, even a soft blouse can cause them to melt like butter! Massage the back of your throat as you are relaxing, then this flake out them and set the mood for the passion!

Gender:

They Are ardent fans. They have plenty of physical stamina and this constitutes for the lack of variety from the sexual life.

Gemini Astrology May 21 - June20

Strength Keywords:

- Energetic - Clever - Imaginative - Witty - Flexible

Weakness Key Terms:

- Superficial - Impulsive - Restless - Devious - Indecisive

Independence:

Gemini Are exceptionally independent. They will not be pinned down by anyone or any rules. They need to experience the world by themselves. Change and freedom are all vitally critical, they will never let them dictate them, they are quite independent, and freedom is essential with their mental wellness.

Friendship:

Gemini Make quite interesting and exciting buddies. They love to leave their mark on everybody they match. They truly are extremely flighty and certainly will disappear for an exceptionally long period as they meet new friends and explore new places. But if they keep coming back, they will have fresh thoughts, remarks, and interesting things to share and ideas to teach. Should you want some advice, their the one to ask. They are masters of communicating and they will be able to help you obtain what you desire by helping you with persuasion and excitement, plus so they provide good advice too. Do not yet, bog one down with most of your emotional problems, they do not wish to take care of it because it depresses them and steps in their freedom for those who want too much long haul assistance, encourage and follow up. They can fill you in with the most recent gossip of course if you love conversation. They are very generous with their friends; they are going to spend a lot of time with you and share everything with you. Even though Gemini is just a social butterfly, they always require time to get themselves and which should be respected.

Business:

Gemini Tends to disperse their energy on various tasks and not just concentrate on something thus leaving a trail of unfinished projects in their wake up. In case they had to focus their energy in one place, their cleverness and wisdom would allow them to finish their job with creativity and success. Making a fantastic manager, they can motivate a team with their excitement and energy. They also produce excellent salespeople because their ease of communicating permits them to be clever and create a comeback to anything a person says. They could convince and manipulate very well. They can easily warrant any move they create and explain any activity.

Temperament:

Gemini Have the capacity to react immediately into situations, and as a result, they've an extremely nervous character. They can be compared into a wound-up spring since they try to absorb everything they could about their surroundings at once. The fact that they enjoy various circumstances and people add for their anxiety and so that they have been nearly always wound up. But if they experience boredom and have nothing to research, they obtain exactly the exact emotions, the demand for variety and excitement. This is the duality, always contradictory feelings in an impulsive, excitable package.

Deep Indoors:

One Downfall is their superficiality. Rather than looking deeply into a person's real qualities, they will judge someone by how they treat them. This will lead Gemini to have wrong beliefs of people and can create problems in relationships. Gemini's could get sense of discouragement and moodiness, but they never permit this to be seen with anyone but their closest friends or family. They usually want every person to consider that they are always joyful and doing wonderfully and stress not affects them.

In A Nutshell:

Gemini Individuals are many sided, quick both in mind and emotionally. They are brimming with energy and energy; they are smart with words. They are smart and Very flexible to every situation and every person. Curious and always want to understand What's happening in the world around them. They Aren't just one to sit and See the world pass, they would like to get engaged. This can sometimes create them Nosy; they do not mind their own company! That is only because they really enjoy

Communication, much more than most other scrapbooking signs, they are the greatest social butterfly. They could speak and speak; however, they have fascinating things to Say their conversation is not mindless babble. They have interesting opinions and Thoughts on things and are not afraid to speak their mind. They are always in the know and will be the main one to watch for the hottest juicy gossip. Lacking perseverance, they readily go off topic to research the following idea or idea. Often shallow, and they will form opinions on thing without diving into Them and researching them fully. This can lead them into believing they understand Everything, which they do but their mind is too busy to fret with nice details. Routine and boredom will be the main anxieties. They would Rather be naive then know the unhappy truth, they usually do not want such a thing Putting a damper in their own liberty or positive energy.

Love, Gender and Relationships

What It is like up to now a Gemini Woman:

She Could be magical but dating her could believe like a friendship afterward the true relationship because of her casual character. This is not necessarily a drawback, but such as the casual person who shy away from too intimate feelings, she may be the best woman. Since she is the only real sign of this duality, she supplies quite the battle. One flip side, she wants to be nurtured, composed, and written to and on the flip side, she needs stimulation and novelty. She is very demanding, and should you not provide exactly what she wants, she will be away on the next experience fast. To continue to keep her curious is challenging, maybe not entirely hopeless therefore she is an excellent woman for the guy who enjoys stimulation and a struggle. She's a mate with an instant mind she proceeds to poke and prod in the feelings and also the minds of people that find themselves emotionally slower afterward her, then be certain you are able to maintain to her comedy or you'll undoubtedly be left . She is more likely to keeping men onto a series, perhaps not completely heartlessly, she's evaluating when the guy is well worth her attention and her period, she does not have any time to waste with a boring guy. Once you have got her approval, she could certainly become covetous. The main reason behind her is jealousy would be that when she will open to man, if she infrequently completely opens to anybody, she does not need to risk her being hurt or tricked. If she becomes envious, you are on the perfect path to authentic love! Gemini women are so arousing they truly are worth the attempt, you may remember her forever!

What It is like up to now a Gemini Person:

He also Is just an excellent date - enchanting, witty, funny, smart, talkative, creative, daring, only be certain you can keep him up! Women are attracted due to these zest for their energy and excitement. You may possibly have rivalry to if you are attempting to acquire his soul. Do not expect to acquire him keep him to yourself. He is flighty and orders their or her own personal, He also will not allow himself to be trapped and commanded by a lady. You are likely to become his sidekick, perhaps not his ardent enthusiast. He loves women and is extremely good at persuading them manipulating them along with his cleverness putting them in to bed, he will say whatever to get exactly what he wants. He is the master of attraction. If you are interested in finding a fantastic fling, he is your top option.

The best way To Bring:

Love To speak, that is the very first rule about approving a Gemini. Be cautious about this you speak about overly as they are intelligent and have a great deal of understanding of lots of things. If you're an expert on a specific issue, teach them concerning any of it, you may amaze them as the know-it-all hint is will not normally understand nice particulars about a great deal of matters, they have been too preoccupied to bother to know. Discuss the mind, engage them at a favorable debate however not be overly conservative, so they find that dull. Be loyal and honest, as soon as they have had their hope broken, they generally will not ever have it straight back again. Gemini really are simple currently; they will perform some activity anywhere. Only enjoy a great time, as you would using a friend because that is exactly what they are, a fantastic friend.

Erogenous Zone:

Gemini's Hot spots would be the arms and hands. These are extremely sensitive places and are extremely open a massage and a gentle touch or stroke. Additionally, this calms the high-strung Gemini and calms them setting the mood for fire. They generally love their finger or nibbled, an excellent integration to foreplay that will impair the disposition. Gemini women think it is great if a person grabs their hands and yells it, just like a princess.

Gender:

Gemini Wants to experimentation and sexual activity using is packed with excitement and novelty, trying everything and anything practically everywhere. Perhaps not for the faint of heart or perhaps the timid and snug fans!

Cancer Astrology June 21 - July 22

Strength Key Terms:

- Loyalty - Reputable - Caring - Flexible - Reactive

Weakness Key Terms:

- Moody - Clingy - Self-pitying - over Sensitive - Self absorbed

Freedom:

Cancer Is your astrology sign that is packed full of contradictions therefore when it has to do with liberty, they could or cannot be independent. On the other side they possess the ability and drive to complete what ought to be achieved they truly are self-explanatory and do not require to rely on additional people for your physical and material matters in life. On the flip side, they rely on individuals for emotional support and reinforcement. The one which isn't fully self-actualized will probably require the steady support of many others and won't be that independent but usually the one who is 'evolved' and contains precisely exploited their psychological problems will probably be tremendously successful as a different individual. They crave attention and relaxation from different folks and so they truly are happiest if they have a small, close knit band of friends or family.

Friendship:

Unbelievably Loyal to people that love and encourage them, they are that the nurturer of their zodiac and certainly will protect and cherish anyone for quite a while. Certainly, one of the most significant things concerning Cancer is the capacity to make the others feel good about themselves and adored. That is only because rather than achieving so for themselves, that they project this onto other men and women. This really is a good cycle as for making the others feel engineered, desired, and adored, they in exchange feel-good in making somebody feel well. Additional folks may lean and rely on them they may hear people's issues and let them nonetheless they will rarely express their very own profound feelings to anybody. Individuals who would like to share with your profound emotional thoughts and remarks using a cancer may believe that the scales have been tilted using both sides and may scarcely show its true profound feelings. A pal is typically a lifelong buddy which may be trusted.

Business:

Once Cancer solved their emotional problems like shyness and bitterness, the powerful personality will shine though, there is almost nothing that they cannot do. They've incredible perseverance and can endure for whatever they believe at. Together with their strong intuition, sensitivity, powers of monitoring and intellect, they are going to have amazing success in whatever they tackle. They truly are exemplary businesspeople and investors due to the intuitive and psychic ability and their creative forward-thinking mind they can predict upcoming trends. They bring riches nicely and understand where to make investments. Cash and financial wellness are essential Cancer, which may help their drive-in business. They require financial security of course should they let themselves correctly focus their energy and do not allow their emotions overtake them they are more capable of receiving their fiscal targets and become exceptionally successful small businesspeople.

Temperament:

They Are complicated, delicate, unpredictable, temperamental and require continuous support and reinforcement, significantly more than every additional astrology sign to become needed. Even if all demands are fulfilled, they may be irritable and cranky. They've an uncomfortable, delicate character. Their contradictory temperament gives their character that the crazy mood swings and potential temper tantrums. They can easily be offended and can sulk and wallow in self-pity for quite an exceptionally long period whenever they become hurt.

Deep Indoors:

Additionally, it Is tough for cancer to start and have a snug mentally satisfied relationship with someone as they are therefore shut off mentally and physically into the globe. That really is driven by their anxiety about confidence and have a challenging time trusting people. This induces developed bitterness and anger in, the contradictory temperament really requires a toll to these and so they may truly have a poor outlook in life, believing that life is simply way too much and gloomy. That is regrettable as when good experiences can be enjoyed, they have been doubtful about people and their surroundings plus so they undergo tunnel-vision because of their gloomy outlook plus so they overlook out the fine things and joyful adventures in life which make it worthwhile living. Along with absence of hope for people, they are deeply sensitive and easily hurt, so this really is why they have their shield shell set up to prevent getting hurt by other people. Cancer resides from yesteryear. They hold beyond events near to them and frequently live on the past. They need to learn how to go and reside at the gift as opposed to spending their time sick of nostalgia. Cancer features plenty of psychological problems to deal with but as soon as they overcome this massive hump of jealousy and insecurity, there is absolutely nothing that they cannot do. Together with their strong intuition, sensitivity, powers of monitoring and intellect, they are going to have amazing success in whatever they tackle. Constantly feeling, emotions and feelings are hallmarks of the hint, which is the origin of their issues, humans are not as improved from the emotional field and this is where they have the brunt in their own problems. They are the individuals that need to manage with their strong feelings so then every additional sign. Once correctly emptied, there is not anything that is this powerful astrology hint cannot reach. Harmony is extremely crucial; it keeps them all happy. Conflict of any type causes great distress. Deep indoors, Cancer can be quite a powerful sign they will have the capability to operate for whatever they think is right and so they will have a great deal of perseverance and certainly will be OK in their own given they don't really allow their emotions get the best of these and also have the firmness that they want. They are not partial to change nevertheless they are able to complete what must be achieved, they are not pushovers or idle men and women.

21

In A nutshell:

Cancer Is a mysterious hint, full of contradictions. They need security and relaxation yet seek out brand new experience. They are quite valuable to many others but occasionally can be indifferent. Cancer comes with a compelling, strong character which will be readily hidden under a serene, and trendy outside. The crab is Cancer's judgment creature and it suits them they can turn out of the shell and struggle however they are also able to hide within their shell of skitter back into the depths of this sea. They truly are extremely unpredictable. There is obviously something that matches the attention because they truly are always partially hidden beneath the casing. They are a have a profound mind and instinctive mind that is hidden in the globe. They are deeply sensitive and easily hurt, so this really is the reason they've their shield shell set up to averts getting hurt by other people. They are nurturers in order that they surround themselves with people, whom after a little while may violate or hurt a cancer before knowing they did thus, for that reason Cancer's protective casing keeps them safe out of harm. They are more complex, delicate, unpredictable and need constant support and reinforcement, more than every additional sign, Cancer must become needed. Once they receive the service they desire, it is an enormous amount to offer in exchange. When cancer becomes damaged, they are inclined to sulk in the place of facing that the men face to face. This prolongs the pain and discomfort. Being very stern, not simply with material possessions but together with people also. Always planning to remain in contact with old buddies and anybody who has been near them, since it really is simpler to keep up a friendship subsequently try to learn how to trust a fresh individual. It really is simpler in this means to allow those mentally. If you befriend them, then you will always be friends for quite a while. The ideal mommy, this really is the indication that symbolizes motherhood. They've unconditional caring and love so then every additional stone hint. Most of the psychics of earth are Cancer. They've an exceptional memory and so are extremely observant and will read people well. They could usually tell of different people's goals are not. Never attempt to mislead them they could see your own motives. Cancer features plenty of psychological problems to deal with but as soon as they overcome this massive hump of jealousy and insecurity, there is absolutely nothing that they cannot do. Together with their strong intuition, sensitivity, powers of monitoring and intellect, they are going to have amazing success in whatever they tackle.

Love, Gender and Relationships

What It is like up to now a Cancer Woman:

She will Be an extremely sensual woman with profound feelings and enthusiasm brewing within the outside. To accomplish these will take patience, time, and tenderness. Do not have a much up her open for you away and jump into a relationship. She will not make the initial movement and will not be ahead of you personally, you have got to accomplish all the task. Do not attempt and guide her on because she is incredibly pleased with a men motives and she will see all the way through you. Trust is probably the single most crucial point to her. If you ever betray her hope, you may also proceed. She needs love and security. Cancer could be the best woman for that guy who would like to sweep a woman off her feet together with love. She is sensual, sensual, and flirty plus you will take part in a tender, flirtatious dancing together whilst the relationship assembles. When there is a sound, stable base, the wealth of this relationship will emerge. She's old fashioned, sensual and feminine and patient, in the event that you're the guy who is able to give her exactly what she really wants, a relationship might possibly be healthy and rewarding and may endure for a life time.

What It is like up to now a Cancer Person:

He also Aren't led with you. He will approach you carefully and slowly. He will soon be quite flirty and intimate and endeavor to court and win your spirit with lavish gifts and care. The rationale he will not be led with you personally will be he includes a strong underlying anxiety about rejection. If you want to know more about a Cancer person, then you will likely need to help make the initial move and have him to get a day. He falls in love and certainly will cause you to his world. Once you "participate in him", then he will continue for you personally and will turn out to be very jealous and possessive. That is only because he is worried, he can lose one to yet another guy and that might beat his soul. He needs one to become loyal and loyal because he is the exact same, at a powerful and intimate relationship, they are probably the most loyal of their astrology signs. They create exceptional fans to your tender woman who adores love and becoming swept off her toes. They are very affectionate and targets holding hands all the time, and constant bodily touch since he communicates the circumstance and adventures with his or her feelings. He is about feeling. He might not reveal it and could depict a calm and cool outside however under, he believes profoundly and profoundly. Could often be readily offended, therefore do not jokingly make fun of these because they will need crime and get hurt, but more, this will not be understood for your requirements. He will only rely on their time he attempts to determine and interrogate exactly what you really said. They truly are exceptional male guards and therefore are like the knight in shining armor. If you are the sort of woman that enjoys being taken care of and cared for, and loves affection and dedication, this romantic, sensuous guy is ideal for you.

The best way To Bring:

Now you Needs to be led. Allow your emotions for them be understood, this may be the first move to starting a relationship. In this manner they are not going to need to risk rejection, yet a lot of the main fears. If you are interested in finding a brief fling, be directly with them. Do not lead them to believing there is certainly long-term devotion is that there was not any as you will hurt those mentally delicate men and women. Trust could be the most essential. Build trust together and so they are going to gradually get closer for you. Let them have compliments and approval but be cautious because they will readily feel whenever you are complimenting them for the sake of it. Be honest. Ask Cancer for information, talk about your issues (but do not burden them) they like helping people and giving information. They enjoy lavish and culture adventures. Simply take them to your museum or play and a fancy, upscale restaurant. Do not induce ourselves right to a relationship or create them decided immediately. They will shy away from you personally. Take patience, here may be the best technique for bringing you. Be physical using these, and they love affection. They have been extremely attentive as well as passes, they are going to slowly grow nearer for you and you will have excellent, fulfilling relationship.

Erogenous Zone:

The Greatest erogenous zone could be your torso and the breasts. Both males and females respond well to moderate licking and sucking of their nipples. You must caress these regions finely and gently. Never be demanding. Stroke your palms through the guy's chest, lightly and softly this will spark the fire fire concealed behind the casing

Gender:

Cancer Is quite physical. Expect sex with for a surrounding sexual encounter. A great deal of tender massages, massages later, candles decorated with the bed side, smooth music at the backdrop, yummy, scented pot pour, what things to appeal to all perceptions. It is likely to soon be delicate and enthused as well as also an event that you will not forget. Do not expect a lot of experimentation and novelty because Cancer can be an incredibly conservative hint. Many folks may be eager to try out something brand new however they will not ever be those to indicate this, you need to, or it is going to never transpire. They may move as well as your idea only because they do love new adventures. Make sure they are consistently feeling secure and safe if buying something new and so they may think it is great and incorporate it in your routine sexual life.

Leo Astrology July 23 - August 22

Strength Key Terms:

- Sudden - Ambitious - Generous - Loyal - Encourages

Weakness Key Terms:

- Pretentious - Domineering - Melodramatic - Stubborn - Vain

Freedom:

Leo Is quite different but they require something to restrain and somebody else to respect them and love them. They have been totally capable to be heavily successful in their however they are much happier when they have got an audience and a few those who appear for them. They would like not to function lonely.

Friendship:

People Are drawn for their own zest for their hot soul. They will have the capability to lift one's spirits and supply reinforcement when they are rough. Their excitement brings people, they truly are social butterflies, maybe not because they would like to be because people always inherently descend and encircle them. Exceedingly difficult folks to not enjoy, they are typically quite balanced, realistic individuals. They dwell before and they will believe you are strange if you are doing. Many Leos may possibly be overly swept up in themselves and be very self-centered nevertheless they are never overly self-absorbed to aid anybody who needs it. They exude their buddies and treat them well also is your greatest friend. They usually do not have a grudge and they are quite forgiving. They will have respect and comprehension of people's differences.

Business:

Business Dealings are simple and powerful for Leo, even if they are in control and command. This may result in conflict at work if they're in a place of excellence, however they generally arrive thanks to their own powerful drive to ensure success, to put it differently they truly are exemplary leaders because that really is their own realm they must get a grip on, plus so they get it done well. Leo comes with a remarkable power to go together with people and so they work best at an organization instead of independently. They are sometimes quite diplomatic in an organization setting and will assign people well, nevertheless Leo will not carry orders. They will need to supply requests but using their own excitement and cheerfulness, other individuals do not need a problem accepting orders from some them as they have been never condescending plus, so they treat the others with equality and respect. Leos are packed with play, flair, and extravagance and this reflects in the world of business. They create a direct effect; they change lives at work and help keep the items moving in Sync and iron out some issues before they appear. In case the company fails, then so that they neglected, and they are acutely determined never to neglect. Leo has turned into really the most extravagant sender of most astrology signs. They will not overtake action however they will encircle themselves with lavish as far as feasible. They will not ever be satisfied with 2nd best.

Temperament:

Leo Loves the newest and exceptional, they hate dull, everyday patterns of course when it is this that they are confronted with, they are going to simply produce their own excitement and drama. That leaves them more likely to liven up a position out of left field only for something to maintain their lively character fulfilled. Possessing a remarkable power to rebound from some feelings of grief or regrettable events, they don't like to become miserable, it hurts their pride in order that they may take things in their hands and make things straight again. Leos may encounter battle with additional powerhouse type of men and women who won't simply take orders, but not to give an inch will not reevaluate their view they are going to comprehend and accept remarks of the others however they usually do not take well to visitors to attempt and enforce their faith to them. Leo most usually have the character of a demanding, spunky kid but this really is just shown if someone steps on the bounds of these own kingdom. They react in this manner because of these territorialities.

Deep Indoors:

Leos Are excessively sensitive but they also hide that nicely. Leos love compliments and flattery, their egos require respect and adoration, it is about pride. This could result in them to be egocentric nevertheless also the warmth of their center keeps it in order. In case Leo's crowd (otherwise referred to as their own friends) don't offer the needed appreciation, so they are too proud to require it and so they are going to undergo a hurt self, however nobody could possibly understand and they'll suffer alone. The trick is they must get needed.

In A nutshell:

Leo Is your lion, this ideal emblem reflects them well. They have a very kingdom that they demonstration and treasure. These are high prestigious, honest, and incredibly specialized in themselves at particular! The kingdom might be such a thing from job to home to somebody, whatever it is, you rule out it. Leo is center stage and packed with dash, they like basking in the spotlight. Consistently making their presence known. They have been packed with energy which behave as a magnet for some other men and women. The others are drawn to Leo's humor, charm, and exactly what they must express because they talk about matters expansive and very intriguing. Leo will not be satisfied with 2nd best. They desire just the best that can cause extravagant surplus spending customs since they love their life of luxury, and that is too readily warranted by the expansive and glorious Leo! Public image is quite important, together with luxury possessions and manners of life, so this keeps the people image in high status. They will do anything is required to secure their own standing and are extremely generous, kind, and open hearted. When your Leo is swept, they are going to fall back with force however they are not you to put on a grudge they readily forgive, forget, and proceed. Always seeking to get things in the world, they have got larger than life feelings and so they will need to feel as though they have accomplished something in the conclusion of your afternoon. They answer situations using actions rather than sitting and contemplating this, they are not spontaneous but because they look in the future and believe impacts of their activities.

Love, Gender and Relationships

What It is like up to now a Leo Woman:

The First step would be to present her compliments and adoration. The relationship will not ever work if she does not obtain this by you personally. Do not start looking at other women whenever you are with her, and she needs become the only real one in your mind. The idea of rivalry with other women completely turns off her, because she is marvelous and expansive and better than every woman (in her mind)! Be prepared yet to contend along with different people. She brings guys, intentionally or not, due to her amazing personality. She creates a fantastic partner because she supplies undying love and affection also which makes you feel very mood on your own. She is kind and inviting having a daring series, she is consistently enjoyable to be with. Leo woman will predominate, although perhaps not for she needs the guy to lead the manner and provide her desired feeling of acceptance, so she looks around her man. Leo woman is ideal for the guy who is tender and has a solid personality but not overly commanding. She needs a person who is enthusiastic about what in their lifetime and that tries to get the finest in all, because does she.

28

What It is like up to now a Leo Person:

The Leo person falls in love and it usually will not survive. That is only because his emotional fantasies of an expansive and glorious romance immediately develop. Leo man wants a woman who is grounded and Intune with all the temptations of life thus that she might help him maintain his feet to the soil. He can appear to be he's open and casual about love however, this isn't the situation he needs adoration and approval also when he receives this he feels quite deep indoors and can cure her with fantastic affection and also be described as a superb joyous companion. He looks like a stone solid un-emotional king but frankly, he is overly sensitive and painful. He is a lady who provides him not at all a demanding manner however he believes he could be eligible for the due to just how amazing he could be. They tend to be more egocentric but under they are gentle and have a lot of love to provide providing the lady will give him exactly what he wants. He will go on with nearly anybody and pretty much any kind of girl is appropriate to him. The lady who disagrees to him overlooks his flaws (he believes he does not need some) and the lady who does not nag at him may demonstrably possess taste and an opportunity at a long-term relationship. In case the relationship continues, finally she might need to show him he really is not the only neat thing on the planet.

The best way To Bring:

Admiration Is crucial. Admire them and they will soon be yours. A reasonably simple hint to draw since they are quite receptive to progress and come-ons. Let them have praise, dish out them at handfuls because they not think a compliment will go a lot. Even if you are faking it, they still do not really care, the only adore the attention. Be funny, Leos want to be amused and so they want to laugh. If it is possible to make them laugh, then you are good! Leos enjoy the expansive matters in your life, treat them into some lavish dinner or even some cultural occasion. Consistently have the greatest of their absolute best rather than attempt to supply them instant pace. They think nothing is too great to them, they enjoy what chic therefore dress nice and classy, and have a fantastic night around city.

Erogenous Zone:

The Rear is Leo's most sensitive location. Many Leos have a well-defined muscular spine, compliment them while you gently scrape your fingernails out of the bottom of their throat down for your buttocks. They like a back massage or rub due to them is being pampered. Get lavender massage oil and provide them a sensuous massage plus it is certain to create the mood for an evening of fire!

Gender:

First Impressions would inform you the Leo is exactly about the kinky and novelty, but this is not, therefore. They truly are profoundly sensuous and enthusiastic and love posh surroundings, like blossom oils and a great deal of caring physical contact such as waxing and massages. They enjoy gender to be recognizable, perhaps not of necessity regular, however they prefer to understand what is happening. That is only because they also must be the greatest of course, when there's a hint or something offered they will have not achieved previously, they'd prefer to spread the possibility then attempt it and also become just satisfactory. Leo has mastered the motions he knows, therefore do not be disappointed with the absence of novelty and number, since they are particularly good at the things, they are able to perform, they are just the ideal.

Virgo Astrology August 23- September 22

Virgo Power Keyword:

- Analytical - Observant - Reputable - Reliable - Reputable

Virgo Weakness Key Word:

- Skeptical - Fussy - In-flexible - Cold - Interfering

Virgo And Freedom:

Virgo Is just an independent zodiac sign. They are fully capable to place their Intelligence to utilize and accomplish things for themselves. It is possible nonetheless Their narrow mindedness induces their ingenuity to suffer and, they can Lead regular regular lives. They could live too much previously and over Complicate things which might limit their capacity to proceed and confuse themselves. In Summary, Virgos can function as independent however the not as Evolved kinds could have difficult when somebody is not there helping them to realize More and perhaps not be quite as significant of these.

Virgo and Friendship:

People Look-up to Virgo for friends as they are straight leaders and resolve problems logically. They have been honest, determined, and loyal. A few people may find them emotionally isolated because they are now living within their minds, maybe not inside their own feelings and emotions. It may be challenging to pin down the way the Virgo friend is atmosphere simply because they readily reside in refusal. Someone who is equipped to learn deep in to still another individual will see if Virgo is not well, but should they face them about it, then they would prefer to escape then speak about any of it. It is ideal to maintain your psychological space out of your Virgo friend unless they start as much as you. Virgo may possibly decide to try to test and restrain a friend's lifetime but just with the concept that they will enhance their lifetime, not only for the interest of controlling. Be patient with your Virgo friend and comprehend their tips are just to create your own life simpler.

Virgo And Company:

Virgos Are very clever, they will have a superb memory and an extremely analytical mind. This leaves them good researchers and investigators. Additionally, they have the capacity to research into an individual's emotions and so they could frequently see into people and observe exactly what their motives are. This leaves them great policemen or even interrogators. Virgos are extremely good at problem solving, so this really is just what they perform best. They are faced by an issue; they are going to pick apart the bits and put it together in the appropriate order. They truly are logical members and therefore are proficient at settling different people's disputes and putting them to the ideal path for reconciliation. Any location which needs the capabilities, which really is just a lengthy list, is ideal for the Virgo. They maintain the world to be able.

Virgo Temperament:

Earlier A Virgo plunges to whatever, in the challenge to a holiday idea, they will need to test all the facts and understand all the facts until they dip into and get a determination. This makes them even seem slow and invisibly. Virgo's perception is the reality, mores then other astrology hints. The things they believe will be just what will likely be, even should they really have a poor outlook in life, matters will introduce themselves to be unwanted and they will be quite gloomy and isolated/detached. Should they have been favorable, the exact events which occur will probably be kept at a certain light and they will be a fine, well-adjusted man. A Virgo mind can be just a powerful mind plus so they should have the appropriate attitude to their lifetime to be joyful and powerful. Virgo should get in contact with their feelings, so this is the reason why they usually look isolated or cold. They truly are extremely likely of surviving in denial. They will say that the texture good or what is okay even though it is maybe not. This really is a simple way outside, the 1 thing which Virgo doesn't like to test is that their feelings thus faking everything is fine is a fantastic defense mechanism for not even being forced to have a better look in their feelings. Virgo comes with an erratic and at times shaky character.

Virgo Deep Inside:

They Have to get organized into their mind, sometimes their energy is chosen out of coordinating their mind they will have a challenging time coordinating their own surroundings. They readily look too deep in a matter and over analyze the things they percept. Virgo is tough and tries to always understand more and more. That really is inside their own ceaseless quest to bring about chaos. Even if sequence is got in the outsiders' standpoint, Virgo will not be settled because they have an extremely busy mind that is thinking and certainly will not be silenced. Virgos wish to become of usage, they will need to be essential and important to everybody else within their own lives and in what they are doing. Virgo's major life lesson would be to learn how to rely upon and have trust in the unknown. They need to comprehend that matters in life happen for reasons that is not always proven in their mind, they do not need to always understand what. They will need to understand how to settle down and maybe not over-analyze a circumstance or event. Deep interior, Virgo is quite sensitive and, they must be valued for all the stuff that they perform. When is Virgo is hurt or offended, they might never reveal it?

Virgo at a nutshell:

Virgo Exists from mind, what is indoors. On the planet, Virgo gifts a serene and collected outside however internally, nervous rampant intensity at your mind, looking to find out things, the way to increase everything, assessing and believing. Virgo can tire out itself without moving! Virgo features a consistent force to improve and flawless, this often leads to extreme pickiness and finickiest. They have been pure; their motivations are fair and so they would like to reach something.

Virgo Love, Sex and Relationships

What It is like up to now a Virgo Woman:

A Virgo lady is introverted, and she could appear cold and blustery, but under the shy, booked surface is located the actual woman, a solid, enthusiastic woman having an excellent convenience of strong loyal love. She will play hard for; she is difficult to get because she is focused on exposing her emotional vulnerabilities and getting hurt. She takes patience and you will need to court and work hard to impress her. Once she is in love, it is for the exceptionally long run. She will be committed, loyal and make you happy as well as put a small sequence on your own life. Virgo woman is conservative and old fashioned, a normal woman who is fantastic for the guy who loves a challenge and enjoys to just take a relationship slow.

What It is like up to now a Virgo Person:

The Virgo person has a trendy outside with a painful and sensitive interior. He is got enormous respect for a female and can treat her equal and like. He enjoys lady who snore his feelings since he is loath to express their or her own feelings, that he attempts and this frequently causes battle not merely inside, but it cleans out to the relationship. This male takes patience and comprehension. He or she will not get exceptionally close and thus do not attempt and put in his mind and eventually become intimately entangled, this will make him feel endangered. He is an elegant woman who is not spontaneous or unconventional. He contributes a predictable living and a predictable woman is likely to make him feel safe. He is excellent for your own down-to-earth, traditional woman. He will not be amorous and sweep you off your toes, however he will soon undoubtedly be by your side and start to become very loyal. This individual's sensuality arrives as time passes. For the lady that wants a well-balanced, solid relationship using an observable, smooth-sailing future is fantastic for the Virgo individual.

The best way To Bring Virgo:

Virgos Want intellectual stimulation. Inform them with details and facts. Always work to arrive at decisions when using a conversation, they usually do not enjoy themes that go nowhere, they enjoy conversations to visit an in depth or consensus, or even in the event that you accept disagree. They truly are extremely traditional individuals and therefore usually do not even do anything impulsive or induce them to produce a hasty choice they simply take their moment and think profoundly within their mind. They are not slow, so their brain is working evaluating everything. Do not try to stunt in their mind due to their emotions are just about closed off before relationship is more solid, and they will decide when the period will probably be. Virgos are natural worriers, do not let this reach you. Do not let them have cause to stress because this leaves them get wrapped as a spring. Let Virgo simply take the guide, they prefer to be accountable for what exactly is occurring. Maintain the date elegant and do not be rough, they enjoy calm and elegant environment as well as people.

Virgo Erogenous Zone:

The Stomach region is quite sensitive to Virgo. Stroke it, then circle their bellybutton with your finger, then provide them a mild tummy massage. This leaves them feel ashamed and certainly will help open them a tiny bit. Be gentle, no abrupt movements or barbarous actions such as scratching or slapping, this can startle them and cause them to escape.

Gender with Virgo:

As Time advances, sex using Virgo becomes increasingly more sensuous. These are not the sort of those who will take part in a 1 nightstand, they are too booked and prudish because of this. Expect sex to make straightforward and direct, no elaborate motions, games, or places. Virgo is not an extremely sexed zodiac sign and does not put much importance about it if anything else that they believe gender to be disgusting and gross. Once a relationship is solid, Virgo is ready to experiment a bit using foreplay and techniques however like everything else between a Virgo, it requires some time to grow once all the advantages and pitfalls are weighed out.

Libra Astrology September 23 - October 22

Strength Key Terms:

*   Diplomatic - Graceful - Peaceful - Idealistic - Hospitable

Weakness Key Terms:

*   Superficial - Vain - Indecisive - Unreliable

Freedom:

Libras Prefer to be around other folks, they are about groups and partnerships. They have been happiest when other men and women remain so when other men and women do their job. They truly are idle but enjoy posh ambient and decor. Both extremes may hit a balance and alive on their or her own may have an extremely cluttered place or perhaps a very densely populated place. They could be independent, so they will have the wisdom and the entire capability within but might preferably co-exist/depend others.

Friendship:

Libras Love delight, fresh conditions, experience and the odd. They socialize with folks from many walks of life. They are always up to something exciting and new with excitement, are proficient at getting along with people, everyone else enjoys a Libra. They're about groups and partnerships, they're the glue which hold a set together as they're those accountable for keeping stability and peace and also have mastered the craft of relationships, not simply amorous but firm, personal, and family relationships merely to list a couple. Nobody can observe somebody else's viewpoint better.

Business:

Libras Dislike hard labor, they have been idle with regards to getting their fingers dirty and working on the project. Luckily, their instinctive instincts are proficient at telling them money will come out of. They could develop great small business ideas which are very original and jump to get success, they could begin the concept however they want another person to accomplish the job. Libras make particularly good business partners however perhaps not superior internet marketers by themselves. They've possibility to be a fantastic leader in their own diplomatic manners, however nevertheless, they are only too lazy to do the tough work demanded and climb a corporate ladder. A fantastic means for Libra to eventually become wealthy is through artistic jobs. They are painters, interior decorators, celebrities or writing screenplays or writing. All these are fantastic ideas since it integrates a spare time activity having a moneymaking venture.

Temperament:

Libras Have exceptional instincts and instincts, most of the moment they usually do not expect them and therefore are highly likely to be more under-achievers on account of this easy-going attitude. This does not follow they are of necessity idle; they simply make do with anything that comes in their way. They do not need such a thing badly enough to struggle because of it. The single time a Libra will most likely endure is when your scenario is unjust, the single time that they will surely endure is whether they believe something between them is equally unjust. They require their esteem and their equity, after all, Libra has been doing a lot for different people today, it deserves fairness, right? If this problem comes in to play, they are sometimes courageous.

Deep Indoors:

They Will also be highly likely to cover up or flex their very own feelings to create peace of an organization also to create the others enjoy these. Sometime this contributes to them not really knowing exactly what their true opinions are since they are attempting to make everyone happy. Additional individuals can observe that, and Libras have made themselves a reputation to be indecisive, they simply do not need to hurt anybody's feelings or lead to illness or friction at a circumstance. This rains over within the individual and several times have trouble making choices. Indoors, the Libra is quite insecure, so they have problems with the lack of self-esteem, they have been always looking for something to perform them. That is just another reason they are social butterflies; it is a subconscious attempt to get the lost peace through other men and women. By attempting to appease different folks all of the time they do not know they have been indoors and urgently need approval and love, they'll perform exactly the favors which people ask and also have trouble saying 'no' or' 'I am too busy' in order to establish how fine they are, that gradually accumulates bitterness and negative self-esteem problems indoors. Indecisiveness results from panic, their fear that the incorrect decision is likely to create all come crashing down on them and lead to chaos within their own lives. Life is like the Libra that admits that life has pros and cons is going to soon be emotionally wound upward, perhaps not hard on themselves so that consequently, they are a far happier person.

In A nutshell:

Libras Would be the diplomat of this zodiac. They can put themselves into the shoes and see things through another individual's standpoint. They truly are those which consistently wish to get things have balance and stability within their lifetime, their own surroundings along with the lifestyles of those individuals near them. They've attractive charm, elegant taste plus they are simple to enjoy due with their eager-to-please, easy going nature. In substitution for a Libra's fantastic capability to become a particularly good listener, sooth, and serene people, they expect appreciation. They will gather a set, everybody else will eventually become friends then your Libra will undoubtedly be at the middle of their group. They enjoy the eye and the appreciation for those people who they have attracted together. They have been extremely intelligent; they frequently hide this of their easy-going exterior. They say their own intellect throughout imagination, many participate with artistic or artistic pursuit. Lots of men and women overlook exactly how intelligent a person happens to be. When the others visit that a Libras wide selection of hobbies and interests, their wisdom and imagination will be more then obvious. Libras like variety and distinct scenarios. They welcome shift. They love luxury and can spend a lot of income and surround themselves with beautiful ideas and so they appear to be always fussing over their look. They love whatever classy and upscale. Al: manners working hard to educate the others, this they perform as many others see them exceptionally attractive.

What It Is Like to Date a Libra Woman:

Libra Woman is charming and enchanting, she is the master of this craft of attraction. The surroundings is critical, be certain that the very first date is somewhere tasteful and classy with chic environment, such as lunch for a stylish bistro afterward the walk across the tree lined paths of a ravine at summer time with the blossoms blooming. She will feel in calmness and think it is great. Give her compliments and tell her just how much she is valued. She could respond bashfully but using each compliment, so the glowing shine inside her will shine brighter and brighter. Once the preliminary attraction has ended with and the relationship is becoming more stable, she will stop her sweet hot manners, perhaps not because she is got lost attention, but it really is because she is idle in love. She could desire a couple of days off with no, this can be like pressing the reset button to the relationship. Be romantic with her and she will not shed interest. Be radically romantic, sweet love notes tucked inside her pocket, blossoms, these matters bring great happiness into the Libra woman plus so they make her feel truly special, that will be basically crucial to this Libra woman.

What It Is Like to Date a Libra Person:

The Libra man is quite popular with women because he is bewitching, harmonious and will associate solely to women within their degree - a feature of Libra is your skill see the entire world through the eyes of the others. They often try so to purify the woman and it consistently works. He always looks looking to find the ideal ladies, regrettably, that will not exist. The nearest thing that an ideal woman could do would be love and become in awe of the stardom. Look as much as him, respect him, he is a sucker for flattery. Do not snore or select his inability to produce a determination, it only will put pressure on him. You decided whether he could not, he will cheerfully move with you personally and profound indoors will probably be glad you just took charge.

The best way To Bring:

They are Simple to draw, they have drawn you with their easy-going nature. First, admire and decorate them. Treat them just like a princess or prince. Libras want to talk; they may discuss such a thing but are especially curious about themselves. Want to make a lasting impression? Ask questions concerning these and discuss their interests, hobbies, and whatever else about them. Though they are diplomatic, they like watching things from different points of perspective. Take part at a light debate concerning a concern investigating either side and the dialog is likely to stream. Dress fine, maintain the air upscale and chic and wash your house before they come on to the very first time. First impressions are lasting. Have a great time, be yourself, you are nearly guaranteed a fantastic time using an easy going, enjoyable Libra.

Erogenous Zone:

The Lower rear has become easily the most sensitive region in a Libra. Caressing it gently or even slow dance will enhance the sexual encounter. They truly are normally very partial to a light pinch or slap the buttocks.

Gender:

Gender Is enchanting, sensual adventure, just like a sex scene from a picture. Tons of gentle massaging, stroking, caressing. They create highly creative and creative fans. They have been proficient at everything they do, and they are eager to try out something brand new. Continue to keep it classy nevertheless, Libras are maybe not merely one for bathroom stall gender. Set the mood with a lot of teasing foreplay and make ambience using candles and scented massage oils.

Scorpio Astrology October 23 - November 21

Scorpio Power Keyword:

- Loyal - Passionate - Resourceful - Observant - Dynamic

Scorpio Weakness Key Word:

- Jealous - Obsessive - Suspicious - year-old - Unyielding

Scorpio And Freedom:

Scorpios Are independent. They can reach whatever that they put their mind and they will not stop trying. They have been totally worthy of being independently. They are not social butterflies such as any different zodiac signs and some would rather call home in this manner there is no matter of who controls the things in home, they prefer to stay control.

Scorpio and Friendship:

Relationships Using Scorpio are always complicated, exactly like the individual, their own relationships really are a succession of extremes, so they could also be downright moody for no apparent motive. Scorpios are famous because of their possessiveness and jealousy however on the flip side, they have been quite loyal. Scorpios have a superb memory and along with a chance to let things move they holds a grudge against someone who did them hurt indefinitely, in fact a Scorpio infrequently if not forgives and forgets. They may also go up to purchase vengeance on the individual. On the flip side, they are going to remember a type gesture repay it. Any sort of gesture into a Scorpio will acquire confidence and esteem that is vitally essential to them at virtually any relationship, either amorous or never. The very best advice would be always to tell the truth with a Scorpio friend as well as consequently, you are going to obtain an awesome friend you'll remember and that will probably soon be loyal to you personally and not ever make false promises. Their honest and shocking feeling of comedy if different than any additional zodiac sign and the Scorpio creates a wonderful, powerful interesting friend which may be trusted.

Scorpio And Company:

Scorpios Make excellent physicians, doctors, scientists and leaders, and they have been perfectly appropriate to almost any kind of business which creates a difference on the planet, greatly affects society and people and also a Above all, Scorpio must maintain a power position, that is the reason these careers are appropriate to this Scorpio, all of them require one-person in ultimate control giving requests and contributing to a component of people/practices. In industry, Scorpios tend to readily gather riches, they create highly intelligent business decisions and they are quite conservative about spending their cash. Scorpios are famous in earning profits and concealing it, they won't declare it because of fear others may take exactly the exact same path and learning to be a potential competition, or worse make an effort to make use of the Scorpio with their advantage to make use of them to get his or her money.

Scorpio and Temperament:

Scorpios Are exceptionally ambitious, insistent, and determined that will be exhibited by way of a power hungry and controlling attitude. Perhaps not at all a tenacious sense but just because a Scorpio will get the job done with whatever they desire, and control will probably be warranted explanations. It can be obvious to some onlooker. Even a Scorpio never gives up, they all have been so determined to accomplish their objective. The trick to the success is that their flexibility. They can re survey a circumstance and require another approach if needed. This leaves them very versatile and flexible. Scorpios are ferocious competitions, together using their powers of monitoring and their memory that is excellent, they are going to remember facts so when necessary, bring them into the dining table during the right time of need. They will win, with proper arguments and facts to guide their own ideas and opinions. Scorpios are exemplary in restoring order into a disorderly situation and they are equally as effective at manipulating to their greed and benefit. Even the un-evolved Scorpio is really a dangerous person only because they utilize their powers to gain just them and measure on other individuals to fulfill their own desperation.

Scorpio Deep Inside:

Scorpio Is the misunderstood of most astrology signs. They are all about strength and contradictions. They prefer to know about a circumstance and always understand what's happening, figuring out this of their mind, on the flip side, they want to know more about the occult, the paranormal, conspiracy theories along with other kinds of similar puzzles that are unknown. They have been extremely capable of concealing their true feelings and motives, they frequently have ulterior motives or perhaps a hidden agenda. Scorpios are about hands; they will need to take control in any way times. To be outside of hands is very threatening, dangerous into this Scorpio's mind, once they restrain, they feel safe. Scorpios have become emotional, their feelings have been intensified, both decent emotions and bad. Negative feelings of envy and bitterness are hallmarks of the tumultuous astrology sign. On the opposing hand, Scorpios are well-known for their strong and powerful drive to ensure success along with their incredible dedication. Scorpios are always attempting to know their own feelings through locating a deeper purpose in life. Scorpios are extremely instinctive, however, less in a psychic sense, even much more instinctive into your mind they have an excellent comprehension of the puzzle and the power of your mind. Scorpios have a fear of collapse that they keep hidden exceptionally well, if their confrontation never become prosperous their livelihood neglect, they are going to just use their elastic skill to quickly proceed and leave the awful experience supporting. Never expect them to fess up or talk about their narrative by anybody nevertheless because this shows signs of weakness and Scorpio always wins, and they have been consistently the best! Some reason they look like they consistently accomplish their aims is they establish physiological short term aims they understand they are able to accomplish they are aware of what they're designed for which is exactly what they choose for. Scorpios are extremely tired about expecting anybody, an individual should achieve their faith, and this has accumulated with time as soon as most of the 'trust evaluations' have now been passed, Scorpio loves deeply and profoundly. Under the trendy outside, feelings and energies are constantly flowing although also the Scorpio relates to this specific be directing this to useful actions, conventions, relationships or perhaps a livelihood. It really is not apparent to the outside observer however knowing this simple fact explains why Scorpios are so enthused about anything its they are undertaking. Scorpios have powerful instincts plus so they hope their own gut sense that can be just another reason a Scorpio infrequently fails. The continuing lesson in life for people born under the Scorpio zodiac signs, will station their own powerful energy to positive targets rather than resorting to the darker forces in life like greed and manipulation, they are going to subsequently have great success within their lifetime also have a tidy, joyful conscience and also a circle of friends they are able to trust and hold precious for them.

Scorpio at a nutshell:

Scorpio Is the only real indication of migraines and strength. Scorpios are extremely heavy, intense folks, there was obviously more than meets the eye. They provide a particularly good, detached, and unemotional atmosphere to the entire world yet lying under is enormous power, extreme durability, intense fire and a powerful will and a constant drive. Scorpios employ a penetrative mind, do not be amazed when they ask questions, so they are attempting to delve deeper and find out things and survey the circumstance. They always want to learn just why, where and some different possible detail that they could understand. Scorpio's are extremely tired of those matches which other men and women decide to try to play with and they are extremely alert to it. Scorpios often control and restrain anybody who lets them anyone they find feeble. The individual a Scorpio appreciates and respects close for these is medicated with all excellent kindness, devotion, and generosity. On the exterior, a Scorpio has amazing secretiveness and puzzle. This magnetically draws them. They are considered to function as commanding and overly hard but just because they require controller for that causes them to feel safe.

What It Is Like currently a Scorpio Woman:

Scorpio Woman is extremely emotional, very rough, and very demonstrative. She is full of dash and intrigue, an amazing woman who the strong A Type personality man will love, for she precisely poses the ideal amount of struggle with the ideal number of rewards. The Scorpio woman could be your greatest seductive, lady. She will not give a person her heart very readily because she is tired of trusting another individual. The person might need to experience a collection of 'mental testes' so as for your relationship to acquire close and solid. She might well not reveal it, but she is a snug relationship. To this, the person needs to be more trusted, needs to become affectionate rather than attempt to restrain. She is extremely possessive however, that the Scorpio woman is therefore packed with mystery, sensuality, and passion that a lot of men usually do not mind getting owned by her.

What It Is Like currently a Scorpio Person:

The Scorpio Man is like any other person of any different astrology hint. He is a separate section is required to describe dating the Scorpio man. Unlike most other zodiac signs, exactly what it is like to date a Scorpio woman is very much like dating a Scorpio man. The most important distinction is that as opposed to introducing a powerful feminine induce just like the lady, the Scorpio person introduces a strong manly, sexual intercourse. Even the Scorpio person is simple to seduce and get hold of at night, it is a whole lot tougher to develop a true relationship with him. The Scorpio person is overly sensitive and feels lonely and unfulfilled, however he will not ever make a woman understand that. Behind closed doors be sensitive and caring to him interest his own emotions only in the event that you'd like an intimate relationship with him usually do not try to lead him because he'll observe this rather than forgive you. Toying with a Scorpio man can be an unwise move. He will undoubtedly be jealous and possessive and will not ever permit a lady to restrain him. Allow him to take the lead since the Scorpio man is really a remarkable individual, you cannot ever fail when he is going through the evening time! Scorpio men are extremely moody, and their moods change as a pendulum on the clock. Stand with his side nowadays also it will pass. Do not nag him on he has a hard time understanding their or her own emotions. Scorpio men create excellent protections and you may always feel safe under his or her Travels, enthusiastic and lively power.

The best way To Bring Scorpio:

Never be imitation using a Scorpio they can watch it a mile off. Be real along with your remarks and listen to these carefully, (they also have something interesting to say which means that this really is Never an issue!) Do not try to conceal things from them tease them Always need to understand what is happening. Bear in Mind, They're the only ones which can tease and exhibit the puzzle and intrigue! They enjoy frankness and Honesty; talk the mind they will honor that. Scorpios are curious in Just about all tasks, therefore finding something to complete should not be an issue.

They Are unpredictable and may shift span of this date mid-way though take these final second changes having a grin and decide to try something different. They enjoy individuals who are not scared to ditch an agenda and decide to try an alternative. In dialog, don't inform them that their remarks are erroneous or take them down, they're too pleased with this as well as if it's a joke, so they may not go on it with all the comedy that you simply meant. Never try to restrain them but do not be that the damsel in distress, they enjoy strong, real people who have forcing challenging personality just like theirs.

Scorpio Erogenous Zone:

The Genitals are everyone's erogenous zone however as the Scorpio could be the very sexually charged of zodiac signs that the genitals are excessively sensitive and can spark a fervent fire that cannot be extinguished. Stroke and caress these are as gently. There is not any wrong way to excite this area, but you should be gentle.

Gender with Scorpio:

Gender Using Scorpio is an overall physical and psychological experience with both fire and strength. They have endurance and may continue forever, round after round. Scorpio is your only real sign that is the most inclined to behave a sexual dream. Most individuals will discuss it however the Scorpio is going to do it and they are going to throw themselves in the part. Usually do not imply a dream to some Scorpio if you do not intend to perform it! Many Scorpios are strong and direct plus also they appear to be an expert in what they are doing. They keep on seducing you as the action persists. A thrilling adventure not for the faint of heart!

Sagittarius Astrology November 22 - December 21

Power Keyword:

- Freedom

Weakness Key Word:

- Un-emotional

Freedom:

Freedom Is Sagittarius' principle, as they all crave experience and enthusiasm along with welcome change with open arms. Sagittarius is the indication of this bible and the explorer, so they are going to go so far as road will proceed and research every corner entirely inside their eternal hunt for intellect. Freedom is indeed crucial they will make conclusions primarily based on the quantity of freedom that's distributed by the choice they've made, because of this, sometimes a fantastic opportunity is refused as a result of its high devotion desire, however that really is actually their choice therefore it's a fantastic selection for them.

Friendship:

Sagittarius Make excellent buddies due to their reassuring, positive disposition and their kind spirit which may do anything to be certain that the friend is joyful. They usually do not expect favors in exchange, their kindness really is self-less. They usually do not hinder other people's aims and they are never possessive or covetous. They treat others how that they would like to get medicated and life predicated in a 'live and let live' policy, so making them agreeable. They truly are exceptional conversationalists that have a fantastic sense of comedy, sometimes their comedy is your raw truth, however these folks speak their mind and do not hold back anything. The things they say is exactly what they mean, but do not enjoy mind games, so it keeps them wanting to determine what is supposed they enjoy straight-forwardness and expect it in return. Sagittarius are famous for mentioning the 'debilitating truth', however on the flip side, folks know they could trust what they say because they consistently state what is real. They hide such a thing and have become likeable men and women. The only real people which may not go and them are those who live by an everyday schedule with an extremely organized, organized life. They have been highly likely to continually be running and miss out a romantic date, however this is because they are so forward thinking they just forget about the gift. Tolerance is necessary, they do not do all these things deliberately, this really is precisely who they are. If you realize that and accept this, then acquiring a Sagittarius on your own life is likely to make the sunshine much brighter.

Business:

Sagittarius Are created entertainers and conversationalists. They've no lack of ideas due with their daring way of life and exciting life adventures. They create great storyteller, comedians, authors, philosophers, and celebrities to list a couple, fundamentally are worthy of whatever so long as it does not tie them down with a lot of devotion. They love to really make the planet a far better place and also a livelihood which is going to accomplish this really is ideal to Sagittarius, they don't yet enjoy the nice information and everyday day to daily regular that bores them they are inclined to procrastinate and let somebody else handle the particulars. They work nicely in operation things nevertheless they are in their most useful as it really is crunch time. If today is the time for nothing, and there is just a good bargain at stake, so they can find whatever finished. Crisis brings forth the absolute best in these, that they do their best under great pressure.

Temperament:

Sagittarius Are not psychological deflecting men and women, in fact they are sometimes down right mentally isolated nevertheless they really do get irritable if they are bored. They have been positive and optimistic, even deep indoors because they genuinely believe no matter what is happened, something good is around the corner and the sun will always shine.

Deep Inside:

Sagittarius Is a well-adjusted man without the emotional issues holding them. They only desire to learn more about the world, maybe not worry about feelings and emotions. The others could possibly be hurt by their own lack of devotion however they don't really care, that is why they have been around this particular planet they have been here in order to obtain wisdom, learn and research. Sagittarius has issues completing some projects they started in case it requires too long they need immediate success and will proceed ahead into this next job in case it requires too long term. This is not because of laziness; they have been not even close to idle but that motivation to proceed ahead is due with their hate of boredom. Boredom is their panic and rather than confronting it, they are going to up and leave searching for something stimulating. They are not emotional people nevertheless they are often hurt by a careless egocentric action; there will probably be gloomy but transform it around fast using their naturally sunny personality. They do not really live on hurt since it is a waste of these energy.

At a Nutshell:

Sagittarius Be seemingly guided by chance, great stuff happens in their mind and this is often because of these optimistic prognosis and favorable disposition that brings good luck. Despite hardships, they have been always optimistic that things can happen everywhere, and the long run conveys great fortune. They've a brilliant, grand character that is free as a bird and cannot be contained. They are full of fascination and so they consistently anticipate the near future, never dwelling previously. They are isolated from feelings because feelings hold an individual back, they do not like to discuss their feelings they only experience them and proceed. They are sometimes reckless and irresponsible since they are going to jump in a proposal of something brand new until they consider the benefits and pitfalls.

What it is Like Currently a Sagittarius Woman: How

She includes a Fantastic attitude and always looks on the move. Sagittarius woman is to get your man with a great deal of energy and imagination. She enjoys unconventionality and shift, therefore whisk away her past 2nd to somewhere unkind and she will remember you forever. For her to remain, you must keep her happy. When she gets tired or unhappy, she will not bother to resolve any issues, she will only go outside and never return. Luckily, it is not so hard to maintain her happy. Be her friend, she will not enjoy like to badly any way, for those who should be her companion, then love will blossom then. Let her have her freedom, laugh with her, and accept the relationship do not rush. Be honest, genuine, confident, and adventuresome rather than play with mind games. The blessed man is not only going to have a superb fun relationship however an adventuresome companion too.

What it is Like Currently a Sagittarius Person:

This Guy Can be hard to pin down. He adores the trill of this chase therefore he can be away attempting to find different women at precisely the exact same time that you are working to get him. He is true if he says he likes you but that intends it to other women when he informs other women precisely the very same. He is perhaps not intimate or showy, and he proceeds to entice women who enjoy the joy of themselves, that is not too bad of a bet. To win him be little about love, do not engage him emotional commitment like talks about being together later. He could be right for that woman who will not desire loyalty or is fearful to be tied down into a relationship. This guy is ideal for the daring, daring female.

The best way to Bring:

Speak to Them ask them questions about themselves, and share stories, and make them laugh, but usually do not encounter intimate facts in their lifetime. Keep your psychological space plus they will soon be drawn for you. Easy. Suggest a backyard date, something wacky and wild just like drifting on a boat down the river afterward using a picnic from the river side, such a thing. They love activities. These will be the best people to find yourself a date but neglect; t even thinks this is composed of stone; they are the largest commitment phoebe of zodiac signs. Take time you have spent Sagittarius and be ready to proceed or share them with the others since they will do the exact same. Overall good fun.

Erogenous Zone:

The Thighs are extremely sensitive, so encircle the inner thigh or nibble softly on the epidermis. Contain thigh stroking into foreplay and you should have sparked your own passion.

Gender:

They enjoy researching the same using their sensual experiences. They truly are individuals most inclined to possess outdoor sex, or even risqué sexual experiences. They are winners of one-night stands since it seems good and you also do not need to be worried about one other man being clingy after! Together with Sagittarius, anything squeamish and conservative demand not to apply!

Capricorn Astrology December 22 -- January 1-9

Strength Key Terms:

- responsible patient ambitious resourceful loyal

Weakness Key Terms:

- dictatorial inhibited conceited distrusting unimaginative

Freedom:

Capricorns Are very independent since they understand their capacities and consequently, they rarely expect the others to complete details they prefer to do all of it themselves.

Friendship:

The Capricorn could be your robust friend, they are going to be present to help, they are rather sympathetic, affectionate, and useful into some friend in need. They will get somebody back to their own feet with a steady arrange for success also for this they expect nothing in exchange. They are a pal who is mysterious and deep and packed with amazement, there always appears to be something happening within his or her mind.

Business:

Together with A character that is aimed at this of achievement and leadership, they always wish to scale the business ladder as well as the most effective that they are. Possessing a superb awareness of handling and time it nicely, they have been excellent organizers. They are highly creative, perhaps not creative. however, it really is incorporated in their time handling skills and their thoughts for executing a strategy. Capricorns generate good, prudent investments since they go through the exceptionally long run and what is going to soon be the most helpful down the street.

Temperament:

Capricorns May appear sadness and stern since they live by self-discipline and responsibility. They appraise all and so they usually do not simply take fearless chances without contemplating the benefits and pitfalls first. On the onlooker, they may appear boring, but it is the severe driveway and organized means of life they feel protected. Self-sufficiency can be mistook for coldness, they aren't as cold as they seem, as this may possibly be evident simply because they prefer to do whatever themselves in this way there isn't any bother about something perhaps not finished or never done precisely. It is about control in the surroundings and their everyday lives and occasionally this shed into other people's lifestyles. They believe they could provide structure and organize different people's lifestyles too; they are able to others may see that as sensitive and never welcome that the Capricorn's implied changes. As stated by these, there is simply an ideal way and a wrong way to accomplish things along with this idea creates some closed minded, tenacious, and loath to accept other individuals. This is a continuous lesson for Capricorns, comprehending there was more than 1 method of accomplishing things and although their manner is normally right, it does not necessarily mean they must enforce their ways on the others.

Deep Indoors:

Capricorns Possess this feeling of depression and requisite for work and structure because inside they believe that they have been unworthy and will need to always prove their values. Once they recognize they desire is self-explanatory, do or will start and so they are going to observe the world at a brand-new light, the one which enables for pleasure along with guilt-free fun. Their main need is security, financial and material security. Here is the driving force supporting their rough personality along with the other personality faculties of desire to be successful. They have been quite worried about their public status and their own prestige. Capricorns are loners however additionally they will need to feel valued, however they are exceptional at hiding this reality. Often very self-included, they will have lots of faces that they gift on the planet they have been called aloof and indifferent however that will be them hiding themselves out of the Earth, regrettably they might never understand they really are. This induces feelings of bitterness and induces them to question their very own self-love. Capricorns make it tough to become close emotionally as after they let somebody else in, they do not need to allow them to proceed and psychological relationship makes them feel susceptible nonetheless fulfilled at precisely the same time. This is a continuous internal battle of contradictions of his or her mind.

In A nutshell:

Capricorns Are incredibly challenging individuals, they've something that they truly are chasing and, they desire their own lives to become fulfilled as well as crucial. They truly are acutely patient and can wait for quite a while for something they desire, once the chance arises they will plan their steps attentively others, they may possibly seem reluctant but that

51

isn't accurate, but they understand there is just 1 opportunity to achieve success and they're filing their advice to choose the correct measures to do their goal with flying colors, not simply second speed. Capricorns have an extremely busy mind and strong powers of attention and enjoy being in control of the own surroundings and everyone inside their lifetime. Capricorns are extremely cautious but this just to survey the problem before jumping in, they will not ever create a hasty leap. They accept shift but present it slowly in order that they can get accustomed to it and incorporate it in their own life. Capricorns tend to observe life in white or black, authoritative just. There are no grey spots such as all these are areas which are not known and that makes Capricorn feel uneasy. They are normally in hands in an intimate relationship which way they are never exposed to a different individual.

What It Is Like currently a Capricorn Woman:

Deep Indoors, she is amorous and adoring however, it can take the ideal person to expose that. On the exterior, she might appear to be she does not care for love. The Capricorn woman is ideal for the guy who enjoys difficult. It takes some time to get nearer to her, not ever make her rush into a relationship. Show patience because she is. Capricorn woman is extremely tasteful, upscale female. You have got to woo her court her like a female. Shower her with fine gift suggestions (however, maybe not overly pricey, she is an incredibly conservative spender and expects one to be too). She will dominate and control the relationship however in her fascinating subtle method, let us take the lead she will not steer you wrong! She will lead the relationship while in the ideal direction because she is practical and smart. She will give you an exceptionally long lasting, real, loyal relationship with the ideal ingredients for enjoyment.

What It Is Like currently a Capricorn Person:

The Capricorn man is quite physical and enthused, however, maybe not emotional (on the outside). Deep in he gasped for love but that has quite a while to come to be reality, he is very loath to put confidence in someone else. Show him just how much you really respect him and make confidence slowly as time passes. He could be very loyal, the absolute most loyal of zodiac signs. Under his secretive cryptic nature is an enchanting series with a solid lusty side, this side is wholly hidden as soon as unlocked, you are going to be astonished at the transformation that this man has gotten! Patience and hope are vital with a Capricorn person, he is much to offer you the ideal woman who will wait patiently.

The best way To Bring Capricorn:

make Them laugh, they tend to be depression therefore anybody who can create them laugh is valued. Discuss anything but do not rush to their emotions. They do mind playing yours, nevertheless. If Capricorn feels safe, they are going to let a few of these kitties from the bag. Discuss about serious issues, matters that matter, and give a wide berth to unconventionality, they are very traditional people and do not enjoy shock-topics. They prefer to be linked to within an intellectual level. They enjoy gift suggestions, maybe not flashy and costly but useful and practical. Keep it high class, they usually do nothing like second rate gift suggestions, or dates for this issue. Plan an upscale date into some memorial, theatre, or elaborate restaurant. Never be overdue. Capricorns are extremely punctual and live with a program and so they do not prefer to be kept waiting it shows irresponsibility. Show patience using Capricorn, under this aloof, indifferent outside establishes a physical, ardent loyal man which should turn out whenever the time is correct, as soon as you have demonstrated yourself.

Erogenous Zone:

The Legs and notably those knees have become sensitive and painful. Gently emphasize the springs of Capricorn's knees and this also can make them glow with delight and commence foreplay.

Gender:

Capricorns Have endurance, tons of it. They enjoy fine, elegant environment and a cozy setting. From the bedroom, that they are going to endure through the evening and desire a bit more. They are extremely good and physical at the things they can perform. Do not anticipate any creative or zany places but expect it to become good.

Aquarius Astrology Sign January 20 - February 18

Strength Key Terms:

*   Witty - Clever - Humanitarian - Inventive - Original

Weakness Key Terms:

*   Stubborn - Un-emotional - Sarcastic - Rebellious - Aloof

Freedom:

Their Personality is quite independent, any effort to carry down them or confine them may cause them to flee. They must be liberated to be in the own. Freedom is not only desirable by Aquarius; it is vital for their wellness.

Friendship:

Beneath The isolated, unemotional exterior is still a kindhearted friend which may venture out of the way to help the next. They like to make people laugh and cheer up people and making them feel good to get the others feel well. They usually do not expect anything in exchange because of this might place a damper in their freedom they live without the strings attached. They are very unconventional and always packed with delight, a pal that makes life more fun. They may give you a spontaneous eleventh-hour camping trip without an equipment prepared, if you select to go together, you may truly have a weekend to remember forever!

Business:

Aquarius Enjoys accomplishing something useful with their own lives, mixing that using their awesome manner with people, they create great politicians and societal workers/psychologists. They truly are innovative leaders and are proficient at forming fresh ideologies and concepts, any sort of research is quite worthy of them. Their sole downfall at the company universe could be that the focus on detail, so they enjoy the expansive suggestions and gigantic plans and could cause them to happen, nevertheless the everyday day daily insistent details induces them. Aquarius wants a secretary.

Temperament:

Aquarius Often be more rebels solely for the interest of owning their very own way. Their stubbornness sometimes causes their collapse, they are going to carry on to do something their manner despite the fact that the others have demonstrated it's wrong, they have been extremely smart folks and know it's wrong but they'll persist because it's their manner, they're quite repaired in opinion and uncooperative if faced. Despite their own stubbornness and mended opinion, they will not ever enforce their thoughts on the others, they've respect to everyone's gaps.

Deep Indoors:

Consistently In quest of intellect, they're extremely observant and so they are able to gather their advice because emotions aren't getting in the way they appear to become above feelings entirely so when they speak, they speak the facts. Sometimes it might be shocking or debilitating due to the disregard for your feelings of many others, however, they want no injury they call it as they see it and also don't feelings cloud their decision, they have been very isolated from emotion. It is not too Aquarius are unemotional, they simply do not expect their emotions in order that they incorporate them in their thoughts of who they are. Because of this, if somebody does not trust their thoughts, they will sometimes go, perhaps not just as far as the other zodiac signs nevertheless as Aquarius is wisdom driven and never emotionally pressured. Sometimes they wonder whether there is something in life they are missing since they do not feel the same as other men and women feel. This will not absolutely keep them from getting engaged with romantic relationships, they are capable with the however, the individual on the opposite end will always observe a feeling of detachment. Aquarius wonders 'why?" Therefore, much they can question their presence. They wonder whether what they do is of use they need other folks to find them and love them, that results from inherent insecurities which wonder when other men and women accept them because they truly are these really are not attracted to the surface since it doesn't matter how much, they are aware they truly are special.

In A nutshell:

Aquarius Is your indication of both visionaries, unconventionality, and intellectual liberty. They truly are the men and women who detract from the audience and move their own way. They have been always after intellectual stimulation, so always discovering something brand new, forming fresh remarks and traveling their manner no matter of what other men and women think. Aquarius are full of paradoxes they want to know more about the alternative ends of this spectrum, so they all enjoy to be lonely are social butterflies they prefer to have either side and also watch both remarks since they invent new ideas together with their forward thinking, active mind. Using a 'live and let live' policy where everybody else is free to be, never judging the others as as people, many of us are equal and entitled to your opinions. They truly are skilled and incredibly witty, so they detect people and find out to socialize with the others through monitoring. They are masters of exploitation virtually whatever they think or do. Because of this, they could cope with any personality and conform to almost any circumstance. They advised shift because boredom is the enemy. Anything fresh is a chance. Aquarius may function being a specialist in almost any topic, they have been particularly good at devoting their significance, they believe it is deserved due to their eccentricity makes them exceptional. Traditional folks recall they prefer to jolt and detract from the standard, this really is the way they are gone. Known to pick anyone they find feeble or dull-minded. It is merely a simple target for verbal practice to them, no injury is supposed nonetheless it may possibly be obtained from the different individual. Deep interior, Aquarius would not knowingly hurt anybody, they've respect for every individual, thought this could not appear evident to the emotional types.

What It Is Like up to now an Aquarius Woman:

The Ultimate independent girl. She is funny, smart, daring, not clingy or covetous, not demanding and perhaps not too emotional. She is inconsistent and desires delight. Anything goes together with this woman and any man she selects will soon possess an incredible relationship. Court her woo her she anticipates this lady-like therapy, she is old fashioned in this sense but be understood her mind has constructed and when she is not interested, she will never be curious. The relationship will advance slowly because she does not get emotionally engaged very readily and she is perhaps not merely one for gaudy displays of affection. The guy who is hoping to secure her soul must take care of with respect and treat her as the same. Communication is key, it really is the way a relationship using an Aquarius woman evolves. Once she intimidates you and you grow closer, she is a remarkable loyal and kindhearted individual. She will always appear to get isolated; she fears losing her individuality in a relationship and thus you should not be shocked if in a long-term relationship she seems like a fiend afterward an enchanting partner. Do not push her mentally or tie down her with requirements and responsibilities since this can induce her to conduct. Never be covetous, this really is a massive red flag for her, and she will leave straight away and cannot be tied down, so she is free like a bird. For those who give her all she needs, she'll soon be wholly loyal which means that you shouldn't be worried if she has gone outside on her , give her distance and respect her solitude and all will soon be well. Aquarius woman is really for the guy who loves a challenge and experience.

What It Is Like up to now an Aquarius Person:

This Person is about intellectual stimulation. You may be the most adorable girl on the planet, but should you not rouse your mind, he will not disturb. Communication is therefore essential for the guy. Deep in he dreams about love but that induces him internal difficulty due to his inability to know emotion so when in love usually stumbles on their words, show patience with him and do not hold it against him as deep inside he could be having pleasure. Yells he can drop out of love just as readily as falling in love. The lady needs to accommodate to him he will not change for those who and demands understanding and respect for how he could be, however bizarre his ideals have been. He needs stimulation and a partner to share life's experiences with, not simply somebody to take a seat on the sofa and see a movie constantly. Do not press him mentally or tie down him with requirements and duties because this may make him conduct. Never be covetous, this is really a massive red flag and he will leave immediately away and may not be tied. In the event that you give him all he wants, then he'll soon be entirely loyal which means that you shouldn't be worried if he could be outside on their or her own, give him distance and honor his solitude and all will soon be well. Aquarius person is for that lady who loves a challenge and experience.

The best way To Bring:

Communication Is essential. You ought to have the ability to excite their minds, participate in an agreeable, witty verbal struggle but do not expect you will arrive at some decisions, that is not the point. They crave that the mind drill. If you should be not able to maintain with the wisdom and the unconventional manners, he is famous for, then you may like to look elsewhere. Needing communication compatibility then whatever else. Have number in your dates, think about interesting activities to do enjoy a trip into the zoo, however if you cannot consider some mad concept, leave this up for him to create plans but don't be shocked when they change your master plan from the midst, be elastic like these. They usually do nothing enjoy naggers or even complainers therefore maintain the conversation positive and should work well.

Erogenous Zone:

The Trainers and ankles would be probably the most sensitive areas. Most enjoy their knees tied together or held down. They like calf massages along with light scratching your fingernails in their knees and thighs.

Gender:

Aquarius Really have an extremely creative method of gender, they enjoy novelty and creativity, they are not partial to perhaps not fire as well as a psychological sex. Gender to an Aquarius is an enjoyable item, be prepared to laugh and be ridiculous, it is just like an enjoyable game between a couple of. Whatever goes together with Aquarius, they enjoy impulsive experiences and quickies.

Pisces Astrology February 19 - March 20

Strength Key Terms:

- Compassionate - Flexible - Accepting - Devoted - Imaginative

Weakness Key Terms:

- Over Sensitive - Indecisive - Self-pitying - Lazy - Escapist

Freedom:

Pisces Needs a dominant partner of character model in their own life or else they are going to Fall to a pit of self-pity along very readily with self-undoing. Once They are independent and Motivated by life events, their imagination comes shining through nevertheless they truly are Struggling to be in their own for a long time until they start dreaming about their Fanciful environment of happy folks and happy endings. They want others to Maintain them on the ideal path.

Friendship:

Pisces Will head out of the way to aid a companion. They have been sensitive and true. They will require a buddy problem and make it their very own and have problems together with them. This could be actually the weak spot however any pal with the zodiac sign needs to know that even though they have been drawn to individuals who have acute issues who urgently need assistance, this actually does more harm them even good. Though they offer to create everything right, do not permit them to defend myself against your entire issues because they are going to lose their individuality on your circumstance. They desire a solid confident friend to create sure they are stronger. They enjoy experience, new circumstance, and societal events. Even a Pisces friend will have something intriguing in mind also it is quite a fulfilling, long-lasting friendship.

Business:

Pisces Doesn't require well to your place of leadership or higher small businessman, they are exceedingly sensitive and with a lack of self-discipline and inducing self-confidence for a place like that. What they have been great at ISIS acting, writing, poetry, or even being artists and therefore are great at whatever amuses at one's heart strings and mystical/spiritual. They are incredibly creative and may rely on their skills of imagination and their comprehension of visitors to inspire the others. Regrettably, most simply take the quick way out of life without having to reach the amount of recognition they possibly might, they must prevent self-doubting themselves since they have been capable to be good role models and leaders into the others, people do appear for them.

Temperament:

The Pisces personality is tricky to pin down, so it is very cryptic and mysterious. They are modeled with their own surroundings; they feature their adventures and surroundings right into themselves. They've extreme compassion plus also they believe that the annoyance of the others. When something is wrong on earth that affects them, it affects them they go to heart and come to feel extreme feelings concerning the issue. Once they are happy, they are incredibly happy so when they are sad, they are excessively sad.

Deep Indoors:

Pisces Possess an intuitive and psychic skill then any different zodiac signs. They anticipate their gut feelings and whenever they do not, they immediately figure out how to because they realize their hunches usually are accurate. A big downfall is the significance and their inability to reject someone else. They usually do not enjoy rejection plus so they decide to try to deal with others how that they would like to get treated in order that they will scarcely say no to an individual for fear of damaging their feelings. They will help another individual with their issues and prefer to do this since making the others feel well in turn leaves them feel well. Pisces is your only real sign of self-undoing. People born under this zodiac sign are not vulnerable to bad luck and unfortunate events they attract them by over-indulging, laziness, and a knack for picking ill satisfied spouses and pals. They need men and women in their own life who snore their emotions as this lets them practice psychological equilibrium. The inner battle is extremes of nature and contradictory emotions. They are attempting to nail themselves to the true life while their spiritual universe could cloud their vision, they are going to try to flee or avoid a situation rather than facing it. Their ceaseless struggle is always to understand how to make use of their powers and their own creativity at a very positive, productive manner and seeking psychological equilibrium by not giving their feelings to everybody else, they will need to greatly help themselves.

In A nutshell:

Pisces May be the indication of both mysticism, puzzle and the religious anonymous. They reside in two worlds, the actual life, and the mystical universe where they translate what they find right into exactly what they need. They do so to avoid most of the realities of suffering and pain on the planet. They've lots of emotions and texture both negative and positive intensively. They've a formidable instinctive skill, many are involved in occult or even spiritualism. They have been extremely good at understanding people for they will have the capacity to explore the mind and watch behind an individual's motives. Often being more likely to drug dependence and meditating lifestyles due to their ceaseless look for their anxiety about confrontation and never have to improve a circumstance, they also merit medication use by letting it get closer using their 'spiritual selves'. Once they are aware that this is the reason why they are doing this, you will find it simpler to kick your habit. They are not the pushovers which they could seem, they also will have strength of personality and can endure for whatever they rely on and they may perform hard work to get something that they believe at. They are sometimes quite idle but just in things they usually do not worry for. Pisces may be by far the most sensitive of zodiac signs.

What It Is Like currently a Pisces Woman:

Pisces Women are extremely appealing and intriguing. She is a person feel as a guy due to her dependence on a guardian and pioneer. She is enchanting, feminine, and soft. The greatest enchantress. She can see directly through a guy and she is not an easy task to fool, therefore any man better be directly with her and perhaps not lead her because rather than facing him she will only evaporate. She wants to nurture and certainly will give the person requests, but merely because of their particularly good. She will be sure he is eating properly and getting enough sleep, kind of like a mommy nurturing a young child. Everything she needs in recurrence is a guy to safeguard and treasure her and make her feel as though she is wanted and adored. She could nearly be clingy and reliant but not overbearingly. Her partner will soon end up of half. She needs patience and compassion and you need to be tender. Do not poke tease or fun and certain do not deny her aggressively since she cannot stand rejection. She is excessively romantic and certainly will lose herself at the relationship. The Pisces woman may be your feminine nurturer, the perfect woman for that ideal man.

What It Is Like currently a Pisces Person:

Pisces Man ISIS your supreme romantic, the most sensitive man that believes with a lady. Pisces man is the perfect zodiac sign for your woman who cares that guys are not sensitive, this guy is. But he is got this ideal of love that is unrealistic and can fall out of love after he comprehends there is not any such thing as the ideal woman. This gentleman lives on the planet of fantasies and, he requires a lady to help keep him seated. He always appears to pick the wrong woman, or even perhaps a lady he cannot have enjoy a married woman that manner there is not any bother about becoming mentally attached. He is a female who will control him but very subtly. She needs to help him avoid them of bad habits and terrible notions. He needs empathy, generosity, and empathy, cultivate him and he will nurture you straight back. A fulfilling psychological relationship to your strong yet sensitive and painful woman.

The best way To Bring:

Talk About spirituality, the occult, astrology, anything that is out of range of the true life. They are going to easily become lost in a fantastic dialog. Even though they have been brought on by individuals who have acute issues who desperately want assistance, this does more harm them better. Though Pisces offer to create everything correctly, do not permit them to defend myself against your entire issues because they will lose their individuality on your circumstance. They desire a solid confident partner to produce sure they are stronger. They enjoy experience, new circumstance and societal events and is likely to wind up to doing nearly whatever you indicate. Make them laugh, and they have been usually depression and are impressed when somebody gets got the ability to create them laugh. They are not too conservative individuals and thus do not be reluctant to discuss strange or unconventional matters and educate them strange jokes, so they are going to soon be impressed with that. They are suckers for flattery provide them praise and let them know at a roundabout manner that you respect them. Be sensitive, soft, and generous, cause them to feel confident with you personally and cause them to feel great about themselves and will be hanging around!

Erogenous Zone:

The Feet would be one of the most sensitive area for Pisces. Acquiring the feet and sucking toes are ordinarily a well-liked and are certain to have them cooked up and ready for activity.

Gender:

Gender Using Pisces is a psychological and bodily experience, of course, when you allow it, then it is likely to soon be described as a spiritual experience also and are extremely good at, and love character play with. Exercising entirely inside these functions. They prefer to seduce. Role-play that you are in a conventional brothel and make them seduce you, they all love sensual games because they can secure completely involved and lose themselves at the sensual play. Pisces likes risqué experiences and off beat pursuits. An extremely fun partner for anyone that prefer various experiences and real sex.

CHAPTER TWO

NUMEROLOGY

The normal Premise of an individual, who've yet to be exposed to this research of numerology, is the fact that numerology calculations are extremely complex and take a high wisdom for math. Nothing can be farther from the reality. Numerology calculations are super simple to do; nevertheless, the unravelling of all numerology calculations could turn into a little harder. Like some other technical craft, numerology demands training and expertise to grow proficiency.

Numerology Calculations are broken up to two common types: numerology birth and domain. Each letter of this name has a related number having a certain vibration, and such amounts, together side the amounts at the arrival, provide advice regarding inherent skills, an individual's personality, and permit them to create educated lifetime decisions.

We Shall Start using two arrival numerology calculations Life Path Number & Day of Birth Number and utilize Linda Judith Johnson born April 1-2, 1965 for the example throughout this phase.

Life Course Number: The Life Path Number is the simplest of most numerology calculations nonetheless, it is normally termed the very essential numerological number. It is an external influence amount and may help with uncovering deep-rooted skills & abilities, identify personality traits, grasp chances, and reveal your course in life.

The Life Span Route Amount is figured by the addition of the amounts on your arrival together and soon you reach one digit. The only notable exceptions will be numerology number 11 and numerological number 22, which have become strong amounts called Master Numbers. Inside This case Linda's Life Path Number is calculated as follows:

April 1 2, 1965 = 0+4+1+2+1+9+6+5 = 28 2+8 =10 1+0=1

Linda's Life Path Number is 1

Day of Birth Number: This number provides your arrival awarded traits. It might be considered your signature as you travel through life. Even though regarded as the most important of those four center numerological amounts, it could frequently disclose an extremely distinctive skill you might not understand you might have. Again, with a striking number, its own numerology calculation is just the total amount of one's arrival day. From the instance, Susan's Day of Birth Number is calculated as follows:

1+2 =3. Linda's Day of Birth Number is 3

Destiny Number: usually known as the telephone number, the Destiny Number could be distinguished as the "Reason in Life". It gives a roadmap from the beginning of one's own life into the ending. It informs you when to practice prudence when to recognize chances. It is a partisan number and offers a feeling of how "You", by a serious personal degree.

The Numerology calculation of this Destiny Number is situated on assigning a unique number to each letter of one's whole arrival name. This graph shows that the amounts out of 1 - 9 assigned to each letter of this alphabet.

1 23 4 6 8 9
ABCDE F Gi
J K L M N O PQ R
S T U V W X Y Z

From the Example, the numerology calculations of Susan's name could function the following:

L I N DA J U D I T H J O H N S O on
3+9+5+4+1=2-2 1+3+4+9+2+8=27 Inch +6+8+5+1+6+5=3 2
2+2=4 2+7=93 +2=5
4+9+5 =18 1+8=9 Linda's Destiny Number is 9

Heart's Desire Number: Additionally, called Motivation, Ambition, and Soul Urge Number, shows what is wished for in life, and what is wanted in everyday life. One's heart's appetite Number introduces your deepest inner motivations. This number is notably quiet; nevertheless, whenever you learn how to know and spot this, you can unleash yourself to extreme heights of succeeding.

The Numerology calculation could be just like this Destiny Number, but it merely employs the vowels A, E, I, O, U. Many numerologists incorporate the correspondence Y.

Vowels: " I A U I OO 9 + 1 + 3 + 9 + 6 + 6 = 3-4 3 + 4 =7

Linda's Heart's Desire Number is 7

That you Have the numerology calculations to the 4 fundamental numerological amounts. Bear in mind that studying a single number can prove to be of use; yet, the power of numerology is sold with studying an entire numerology graph and seeing the way the amounts correlate, and also the way they could be embodied to your own life.

My information Is simply begin moving. Play the numerology calculations in your name and birthdate. Do a little exploration and see what the statistics mean. Once you set a simple comprehension of numerology, develop it just like some other technical skill and utilize it to alter and enhance your own life outside what you envisioned.

In Straightforward provisions, numerology can be an evaluation of amounts through the duration of your daily life. You can show data around the globe and every different individual using Numerology. Numerology is an all-inclusive terminology of amounts.

On the Off likelihood you realize about Astrology, in the time you will know a bit about Numerology; it really is relative in a substantial number ways nonetheless uses a different strategy to find the understanding and data: Amounts.

Numerology May be the risk that the world is a frame as soon as separated we have been left with all the essential components, that will be amounts. These amounts will subsequently be effectively used to assist people with bettering understand the entire world and ourselves as humans.

Detecting Meaning in Numbers

Numerology May be the risk that the world is still a frame; once divided we have been left with all the essential components, that will be amounts. By recognizing that everything on Earth is at the mercy of, and certainly will liken into amounts, a numerologist could take a lot of components of a person and divide them to crucial numbers through different practices. These amounts will subsequently be equipped to be properly used to assist people with bettering understand the entire world and ourselves because people at which you are able to come across pieces of understanding of your motivation and personality faculties by working things out such as your lifetime manner number, articulation hearts and number desire number one of others.

The craft of numerology is dependent upon the smoothness of amounts.

Numerology Assessing their nature and vibration, and the way they could be effectively used to readily grab and your overall surroundings. Your likely never considered amounts since with a personality, yet at case you believe about these as somewhat, you are going to know that the larger part of individuals have inclinations for many amounts' others. You repay on those conclusions as you are feeling instinctive admiration for the type or personality of a number or amounts.

What Exactly Is Tamil Numerology?

Tamil Numerology, along with other numerology frameworks (Chaldean, Pythagorean, etc.) Was created as a means in the way to celestial somebody's future, find personality faculties, inspect the vibrational features of baby titles and read through the symphonious samples of planets and their relationships with another (crystal), within such a fashion trying to grasp the feel of "facts" we encircle ourselves inside. During research, documentation and perception, numerologists have toiled to grow an exceptional comprehension of this world and our place within it.

Tamil Alludes to the province of Tamil Nada. Indian numerology says you will find 3 amounts connected to each person...

Inch. The initial number is that the mysterious amount. Back in Tamil numerology, the mysterious number corresponds into the style by which you view yourself and can be set utilizing your debut into the entire world.

2. The 2nd amount in Tamil numerology Is the destiny number. The destiny amount informs how the world sees you and can be dependent on like the amounts on your debut into the entire world together.

3. The 3rd number is your telephone number. The Tamil name amount frees your relationships with the others and demands a scientific count determined by the noise frequencies of a number.

Think about We divide the quantity 6, limited to a version...

In Indian Numerology, the Title no 6 is really a strong number, fixating in your home. Like a Psychic Number, " is really a vibrant, cherishing number, this means sustaining and thoughtful company. 6 at Tamil numerology is hot, rich, and sexy today and, worshiped with all. On the off likelihood you have a6 for a mysterious number, you may generally be family-engaged, inviting and liberal. From the Destiny Number, the niche would be your same: much love in your front, either for family or also to get the longer stuff solaces. You adore magnificence and you also adore to possess amazing items around you. You produce a home-not decorate a house-and without a doubt, home could be where that the center is.

On the Drawback, you could well not be that informed with money, but being liberal to say at the very least. You might wind up committing a large amount of yourself occasionally when it can be wiser to let your company or comparative completely have the physical exercise life needs them. You may possibly be touchy to inspect and- as a6 - - you will stress overly or spend energy independently than different amounts.

Individuals Who've a6 to his or her Psychic Amount may possibly see subject as their practice this life. Since overseers and admirers of all magnificence, they create for incredible pros, economists, analysts, societal laborers, craftsmanship screen proprietors, film takers, craftsmen, and writers.

Bode well?

Indian Numerology also includes pre-assembled squares, which reveal various geometric cases and accounts, a few which can be discovered in traditional Islamic workmanship.

It Really Is Recognized the origins of numerology return straight back over 10,000 decades, any way nobody knows precisely where or once the specialization of numerology was initially beginning. Proof and asserts point out an alternative range of possible factors, from Egypt to India, also out of Babylon into Japan. At the exceptionally long term, be as it might, numerology would acquire hidden in Greece, made predominant first with way of a Grecian called Pythagoras, the unbelievable mathematician and logician.

Numerology - Chaldean?

You will find Two conventional versions of Numerology about Earth today. They really are the older analysis of Chaldean Numerology determined by the entire world's unique origin language Chaldean/Sumerian (4,000 BCE), and also the Western (so-called Modern) Numerology influenced by the pre-Roman Empire Condition of 22 letters (500 BCE). Both frameworks will soon be immediately revealed and stood outside to provide you with from more awareness on the differentiation of this numerology number crunchers.

Chaldean Numerology depends upon "sound-syllables" (noise frequencies/reverberation) that produce energy, making the vibrational types of the "names" The Western rendition of Numerology failed to ride on the vibrational cases of sound-syllables, but within an over simplified, direct, and also sequential endeavor of amounts to the letters of their Western/English letters in sequence.

Numerology, the antiquated analysis of amounts or the analysis of this noteworthiness of amounts, says that you are attracted into the world using a great deal of special numerical qualities which talk with vibrational examples that may have quantifiable and describable consequences. From all those consequences we can detect our fate, that we are perfect with, exactly what our personality is really like, which is only the start. The numbers of one's name and birth date can reveal you an outline and structure which discover the potential that your lifetime stays.

In Chaldean Numerology, sound-syllables reverted to numerical qualities that comprehend and clarify the vibrational examples which influence your body's physiology and energy procedures, and affect both the unfurling, alive, shifting illness inside our own lives. These vibrational cases are subsequently converted to written arrangement throughout the translation of this speech of amounts (numerology amounts).

The Chaldean Alphabet/Formula appeared under allocates just "eight" origin amounts (numerical qualities inch through 8) into the sound-syllables (letters) of these correspondence collections. The First Sacred Officials appeared under was extended out of 22 to 26 letters from your next million years BCE to oblige the speech varieties because humanity extended external. The Chaldean Alphabet/Formula implemented attributes to ensure that the exactness of all elucidations of those cases of their titles. 1 signature was that the high degree of this quantity 9. The no 9 was regarded as "Consecrated" itself, sacrosanct perhaps not simply on the grounds it had been representative of their very elevated amount of other-worldly fulfillment, but also in light of this undeniable fact its level of renewable energy was more than most amounts. The no 9 would not be distributed outside to talk with a lone correspondence of this correspondence collection.

Chaldean Alphabet/Formula

Numerical Pairing with Letters Assigned

1 An, I, J, Q, Y
2 B, K, DC
3 C, G, L, S
4 = M, D, T
5 E, H, X, N
6 U, V, W
7 therefore, Z
8 = F, P

Unique Sacred Alphabet

(2-2 Letters from the very first letter collection with letters, E, W, and F being contained later)

Numerical Values with Letters Assigned (Sound-Syllables)

Inch (An) Or aleph, either (I) or even you, (J) lengthy, (Q) or qoph, either (Y) or you

   2 = (B)) Or Beth, (K) or kaph, either (ep) or even rash
   3 = (C) Or chef, (G) or gimel, (L) or lamed, (S) or even samekh
   4 = (D) Or death, (M) or mem, (T) or even teeth
   5 (E) Extended, (H) he, (N) or pious devotee, (X) or even trade
   6 (U) Or vatu, (V) or vatu, (W) extended
   7 = (O) Or ayin, (Z) or even Zain
   8 = (F) Lengthy, (P) or pe

The Western rendition of Numerology integrates the basis for this relationship of their orders of semantics (evaluation of written language/spelling), phonetics (outspoken sounds/discourse procedures), along with phonics (sound of letters of the very border letters so) with the insignificant sound-syllable/vibrational reverberation centered analysis of Chaldean Numerology. They appear to confuse the orders of language usage with the analysis of Numerology. Additionally, the Western number frame restricts the sound-syllables of one's own name, also, consequently, gives no thought about the vibrational examples which flow against the energy that encircles your own name or name numerology. Afterward, so-called Modern Numerology gift ideas vulnerability and mistake in discovering and distributing your name numerology.

Present Afternoon Numerology restricts the Spiritual need for this no 9. The present-day framework comprises the"9" from the opinion of one's name amounts that induces a misalignment of numerical qualities and helps to ensure that positive results will probably be confused. They appoint the numbers 1 through 9 into the first nine letters of these letters so and then re-hash this series to the remaining letters of these letters so (26 letters).

Current (Western) Alphabet/Number Assignment

1 A, J, S
2 B, K, T
3 C, L U
4 = M, D, V
5 E, N, W
6 F, O, X
7 = P, Y
8 = H, Q, Z
9 = I, Janine

To Outline how Chaldean Numerology will unravel the hidden code on your Name and birth date, we have produced a fractional plan (chart) onscreen personality Shirley MacLaine utilizing her "Phase" name below "birth-name." This delineation provides you with a glance to her personality traits by shifting over letters to numbers and then applying a scientific recipe to property toward the finished item. Shirley MacLaine moves by her stage name as opposed to birth-name, resounding 100 percent to all those vibrational examples and experiences from this name. The next can be a portrayal of all those nine qualities which structure her own plan.

SHIRLEY MACLAINE

Conceived: Shirley MacLean Beaty
Birth Date: Date: April 24, 1934
Missions in Life and their blue-print Descriptions

- *18/9 Destiny

This title Brings the strength of a general leader and leader, is competitive and devoted to serving humanity since the passionate, merciful compassionate using vision.

- 6 Soul/Heart's Desire

The Sweetheart, protector, boundless parent specialized in family, companions, and individuals when everything is said in action; seen overly corrected along with also together.

- Inch Personality

Moving Forward always at a positive posture to fill as the pioneer/pioneer and clean the street for the others to pursue.

- 7 Purpose

The Purpose will be to educate teaching on all degrees, scholarly and skillful using all the longing to share with your information learned through life experiences and self-awareness.

- 16/7 Life Goal

Only at that Period of life, there's just a powerful impulse to stay a strong leader in hands, while being focused on family members onto a residential degree and on the lookout for simple as being a diagnostic educator, in the time sharing data attained.

Earlier You begin an experience of self-disclosure throughout amounts, it is crucial to fully understand and welcome that the wisdom and data reachable from using their standards of Numerology. As there are just two frameworks of Numerology in presence, one ought to analyze and inspect the components shown to validate the accuracy of their outcome. Now the Western frame could be your very broadly speaking employed frame. Be as it can, the uncanny precision of Chaldean Numerology, probably the exact structure of Numerology understood, has been keeps on being exhibited by undeniable outcomes throughout the usage and application of standards that are logical, improving analysis, examination and appear right into, and consistent constant talks.

Why given the others an opportunity to restrain your pre-determination once you can restrain yourself!

Numerology Enables one to manage your destiny. Demonstrably fate is vague, yet it is recognized to be self-explanatory. Therefore, find your numerology number now and focus on improving your gift as soon as possible.

The best way to Find my numerology amount.

Detecting Your own numerology number can be an amazingly simple process, so you should merely several gains and that is it in short. There are just two approaches, one-by such as the amounts of one's debut into the entire world or two-by involving the amounts of one's authentic name. Think about we explore how to perform this

• Adding the amounts of One's Introduction into the entire world:

Condition for Example your date of arrival is of April, 1980, in the time here really is actually the way by that you need to work out your numerology number 1 +0 (day of arrival)+4 (month of arrival)+ 1+9+8+0 (year of arrival)= 2-3. Next this two-digit number has to be made a lone digit number, therefore what exactly you want to do now will be comprise 3 and 2, 2+3=5, so like this your numerology number will be 5. Whatever the instance, remember in case the after effect of one's very first option will be a figure like 3 9, in the time comprise 3 and 9, 3+9=12, currently 1 2 should be split into 1+2=3, then subsequently the numerology number could be . Continuously re-collect the numerology amounts are from 1 9.

• Adding the letters from your title:

Each Correspondence was assigned lots as signaled by numerology, as

1-A J S
2b K-T
3-C L U
4d M V
5-E N W
6-F O X
7-G P Y
8-H Q Z
9-I D C

Therefore, suppose Your title is Edward, here could be the way you have got to see 5+4+5+1+9+4=28. Presently violate 28, 2+8=10. As I recovered prior to the quantity must take single-digit then it ought to be divided yet again, 1+0=1. This manner, for Edward, his numerology number will be.

That Method of one's own number:

Numerology Number-one: Outstanding power abilities, insecurities, driven, aim situated, solid self-subject, gutsy, flighty, creative, creative, exceptional, leader, one-of-a-kind method to take care of problems, autonomous, individualistic, incredible possibility for advancement.

Numerology No two: You're delicate, discreet, friendly, attentive, political, discreet, real, pleasant, creative, unequivocal, intuitive, stable, cherishing, small and calm. You are kind and touchy into the essentials of all others.

Numerology No 3: You're innovative, socially energetic, aesthetic, excessively positive and optimistic, playful, cheerful, and carefree, rousing, creative, poignant, enthused and elevating

Numerology No 4: You're down to ground, diligent, calm, dull, efficient, orderly, accurate, powerful, timely, reliable, dependable, and more dependable, without any stratagem

Numerology No 5: You create companions effortlessly, you are adaptive and multi-gifted, cheery, and helpful and an adequate user friendly and helper. You have got incredible verbal aptitudes and you are exceptionally powerful, appealing, flexible, adaptive, and curious, gallant, colorful and brilliant.

Numerology No 6: Musician, entertainer, teacher, Profession, craftsman, crafts person

Numerology No 7: You're logical, Profession, participated, logical and advanced, pondering, reflective, other-worldly and perplexing. You are a searcher of truth and an aggregator of insight and information.

Numerology No 8: You're rousing, result-arranged, beautiful, competitive, visionary, liberal, perseverant, pardoning, innovative, cash caked and self-restrained.

Numerology No 9: You're cognizant, worried regarding the progress of this World, cheerful, visionary, eclectic, creative, creative, sympathetic, sentimental, magnanimous, and liberal.

At its Most basic stage, Numerology (and its own specific amounts, as an instance, Numerology two or Numerology 1 1) is an examination, whose purpose is always to expect amounts and to reevaluate their cryptic consequences. Amounts and their frameworks are entrancing the humanity for a lengthy moment. Antiquated rationalists were researching amounts for exceptional significance and had detected superiority plus, it appears that something divine within them.

The History of Numerology

Where Numerology descends from and how it was will be always to a level a riddle, at precisely the exact same manner as other older methods of believing. Egypt and Babylon will be the spot that the very pre-assembled written records of numerology are believed to be.

Additional Proof proves that numerology has been utilized an enormous multitude of years ago Rome, China, Greece, and Japan.

Cutting Border numerology is regularly attributed to Pythagoras, who had been a Greek savant. Regardless of how it is not understood whether he established Numerology, he would a couple speculations behind it which required amounts to an entirely distinctive level. All these speculations are now the point of Pythagoras with the charge for cutting-edge numerology.

Dr. Julian Stanton was truly the man that considered this name 'Numerology'. He additionally purchased attention and fame to it in complex occasions. There's not much else notion about the where abouts of Numerology, it is gotten well known from the current society and can be employed by many.

Just how Can Numerology Work? The Basic Principles

The best way Numerology works is completely ineffectual and for the large part demands a professional numerologist to provide point by point and exact readings. Regardless of how it is possible to without much stretch find your own lifetime manner number and matters such as your own demeanor, personality, and soul request amounts utilizing crucial estimations, the way these amounts collaborate which ought to be interpreted appropriately.

The Idea behind numerology is the fact that the world along with also your own life depends upon your debut into the entire world, initial name and lots of diverse elements surrounding an individual. Together those lines, you can find incredible profundities a numerology estimate may give. Because of this, it will provide regularly surprising pieces of understanding of somebody.

It Really Is Admitted that there aren't any happenstances from the Universe your birthday and name sway the experience you may require as well as your own qualities, moreover, that some require a gander in horoscopes or even soothsaying to interpret signs or fates.

Exactly what a Numerology Reading Involves

A Numerology perusing comprises a slew of computations. All these estimations can enter many different layers of profundity with assorted amounts and combinations of amounts conveying different consequences. Really, even a vital perusing determined by your own center amounts can be exceedingly discovering. But in the same manner that amounts are unending, some body's numerology diagram will carry on being siphoned out of numerous perspectives as a progressing venture.

Finding a Numerology perusing is entirely enjoyable and incredibly fascinating, specially at numerologist.com that comes with an impressive, visual point which goes through the harbor of dividing the 5 center the different parts of one's diagram to produce your graph.

That really is an amazing demonstration for fledglings, also it is in addition suitable for the people who want an even deeper perusing. You start along with your name and date of arrival, they describe just how your completely free numerology diagram wont only enlighten you seeing yourself still assist give guidance on your own life and prosperity using a mixture of one's Life Path Number, Birthday Number, Soul Urge Number, Expression Amount, along with Personality Number.

Your Numerology Life Path Number

In Numerology, your lifestyle number has become easily the most critical number. It frames the assumption of how your lifetime may take. Likewise, it needs to be all intelligent of exactly what your own individuality is or should be since an element of one's personality and attributes. A true presence manner number in addition openings any openings or difficulties that you will face, as any exercises you may possibly want to learn enrooted.

Every Life manner number possesses an alternative value.

It Really Is Dependent on adding the amounts at your entire date of arrival.

To get Example, April fourth, 1992, would be 4 + 4 8. Now the 1992 is split because 1 + 9 + 9 + 2 = 2-1.

Currently You comprise both specimens of 2 1 together as two + 1 3.

That really is the equal which has any two-fold digit amounts that you ought to keep on including and soon you wind up getting a 1-digit amount.

Model: 1 9 Requires 1 + 9 = 10, in the time 1 + 0 = 1). Eventually, gather the 3 and 8 to one unit for the own life manner number such as 8 + 3 = 11.

Sound confused? It is simpler than you would guess.

You can Get knowledgeable about this Numerology adding life and machine manner number consequences.

If you Have determined your own life plan amount, so you would subsequently comprehend what it says about you and your own life. What is more, it is astonishing how accurate only knowing the overall qualities of one's own life manner number is to somebody. This will be the main reason many check out find out increasingly about themselves together with additional shirt to base readings.

Your Expression Number

Otherwise Called your pre-determination number, an articulation number is claimed to dive to your own abilities, wants and human objectives. It might likewise be you mindful of almost any inherent attributes you can convey.

Your Demeanor number is decided by shifting on your FULL initial name (counting any center names) in to amounts utilizing the Pythagorean chart. This form of diagram contrasts some correspondence with a lone digit amount. Now, the all-out aggregate is split to a lone digit amount. From and by the genius amounts are applicable to your fate number and are not diminished further.

Anything Articulation number you're left with comes with a different significance and works in conjunction along with additional center numbers to make a graphic of exactly what your individuality is and exactly what you are about being an individual at the broader world.

Your Disposition Urge Number

Your Soul ask number is repeatedly called one's heart's Desire number in numerology. This will signify a feeling of one's mind, or even genuine yourself. The fascinating thing about the soul encourage number is it usually finds truths in people they merely perceive once per perusing is completed.

To get Example, your deepest yearning number will demonstrate that you hunger for the control. Or again, that you are a lot farther and need an even far more significant amount of gratification. On the other hand, you might have a desire to feel prestigious or idea about... every one of the faculties can regularly sit under the outside and in revelation can be quite illuminating. In any case, shifting the whole path of somebody's own life to detect genuine joy.

The depend Is much like the others utilizing your full name. Be as it can, you merely ascertain the quote of this vowels to find your internal inclinations or wants.

Your Numerology Personality Number

Your Character amount in numerology is decided utilizing only the consonants on your name. That really is subsequently trailed with a corresponding procedure of distributing lots to every letter before adding up them and dividing them for at a lone digit amount or professional number.

The Character amount is really the medial side of you which you empower people to view. So, this shows how the others view you. What is true for the huge majority is we shroud ourselves and thus live under a personality. Occasionally that really is finished using exceptional thought. Be as it might, more frequently than not we try so without even recognizing, or not being totally conscious of it. Thus, it is often very hierarchical to comprehend the way your personality number can demonstrate what exactly you miss or do not manage by behaving the way you do. This manner, it can discover additional adventures to your clinics in a variety of ailments.

Your Birth-day Number in Numerology

In Decision nonetheless in no manner, form, or shape least, your own birthday number stays the solution for your requirements as well as your own destiny. This number is totally based on the evening that you were imagined. Coupled together with your own life manner number and other center numbers this could reveal your blessings skills, abilities as well as if you are able to remembers motivation.

In opinion of the entire day of arrival with the entire month, your wedding number will allow you to understand of explicit gift suggestions and possibly where they belong to your world to offer yourself genuine rationale.

Numerology Can be a fascinating wealth of information which provides anyone understanding to themselves throughout the amounts related together with titles. In any case, Numerology might possibly be be regarded as part of Astrology. What type separates through celestial planets and bodies, Numerology extricates by way of numbers. The corresponding article will reveal 1 section of Numerology: birth-date readings. Birth-date Numerology readings might be looked at as the very nitty-gritty now and stunning exposures concerning you personally.

Numerological Birth-date readings could be accumulated through two methods:

Technique Inch:

To take Each of the amounts in the debut into the entire world you need to comprise up them. Include up the numbers before aggregate of most numbers get to the same digit. It is anything but hard to exemplify; Let us

81

state your debut into the entire world is 11/05/1982, the summation strategy is according to the following:

1+1+0+5+1+9+8+2=27 (Require 27 and comprise both digits)
2+7=9 (The result is 9)

Suppose your Introduction into the entire world is 12/03/1985:

1+2+0+3+1+9+8+5=2-9
2+9=11
1+1=2

The Subtleties from the numerological outline will subsequently utilized to dissect and describe a more mind-blowing method. In the previous version, two is that the number that could discover numerological certainties regarding the average person brought into the entire world 12/03/1985.

Technique 2:

The Second method of discovering Numerology realities is by simply exploring which quantity of this afternoon which month that you were imagined. Each potential date consistently continues to be relegated with numerological faculties to that an individual might be socialized together with.

Birth Dates which fall on dates against the very first of monthly on the fifth of per month have been dispersed the corresponding numerological particulars:

- Should you Are guessed on the very first, you might be thought to be always a feature mind. You have got control, solid will and outstanding certainty. You can be strong today and again. Be careful!
- Should you Are guessed on the 2nd, you are extremely delicate, compassionate as well as excited. You have got condition of mind swings today and then; a little strange.
- Should you Are imagined on the next, you are sure, have lots of energy, and therefore are extremely lively. You have got incredible adaptability in every manner; you are considerably employable.

- Should you Are guessed on the fourth, and you are incredible in association and overseeing. It may be significantly stubborn, nevertheless.
- Should you Are guessed on the fifth, you are a wonderful author and are all knowledgeable. You would prefer to never stay static in 1 area for an extended period.

I have got Referenced that Numerology and Astrology share unites using their celestial bodies, but there are always a couple disputes I should refer to. These dates have been common for all weeks of this program year: as an example, two different people guessed on the fourth of March and the fourth of December will share basic person as as signaled by this date Numerology. That is versus the celebrity sign plan of Astrology.

CHAPTER THREE

USING ASTROLOGY AND NUMEROLOGY ON YOUR OWN

Numerology Is the analysis of amounts that defines your faith in your lifetime; in similar techniques crystal-gazing uses aliens to expect one's future and past. Thus numerology -- just how can it help you? Being the evaluation of their connection among amounts and every different individual, the exam uses explicit major dates commanded by your name per date of arrival and other vital occasions all through your own life to to determine what someone will experience throughout his lifetime .

Numerology Can encourage you at the function you want to foreordain foresee life occasions in advance, as each number linked to an individual features an important significance, caliber, short coming, or power linked to it. Numerology is contingent on the number 1 9 and explicit points are employed to precisely pinpoint the number and person is related to. Those who pursue numerological predictions base or partner occasions which happened or would come about entirely determined by the amounts and go beyond and beyond pick various events in accordance with the number expectations.

Numerology Is the more badly chased by more individuals round the planet which some different sort of anticipation as it-related amounts with future occasions which could occur or might occur. Quite a few adherents partner the amounts with events which happened. At this time when a person visits a numerologist he starts by deciding the amount related to a person and profits ahead to share with the average person regarding amounts which are going to make sure in his lifetime along with amounts that charge be related to antagonism in somebody's lifespan.

Despite The actual simple fact precision is catchy, expectations and conjectures such as time of explicit occasions might be produced out of numerology.

Computations Are performed on the name, indicate, or even short portrayal of this occasion to become anticipated. It supplies a celebration number.

Holding That you are usually the one with all the question, your debut into the year, birth month, birth date, and lifestyle amounts are in addition ascertained.

At that Point, every date out of tomorrow provided a year after on is ascertained independently to comprehend how well the date numbers organize the occasion along with your debut into the date numbers. Each game has a spot respect determined upon the importance of the game.

In this Manner, there are amounts of games. A couple of dates may possibly arrange somewhat. Various dates will organize entirely.

Certainly, one of those Dates together with the top earners could be that the point in that the occasion is on how that occurs, to the off likelihood it does occur by some stretch of your imagination.

In almost any Instance, that you never have to accomplish any one of those figurines. There is an internet apparatus that will all these.

The Planning is not accurate. It cannot function, about the reasons there are many factors beyond the amount of numerology calculations. Rather, the points provide probabilities -- just how likely it is that it will occur on a certain day grapple with happening on various days.

Individuals, who are at pressure and facing a few issues during their lifetime, usually attempt some spiritualist hypotheses to get structures. They try to find out a way to dump their problems and hence they begin with confidence in a variety of forms of spiritualist techniques. Regardless of that numerology is thought for a science fiction, any way a massive section of the individuals seriously considered any of it within an outstanding clinic. Whatever it really is, numerology is helpful for foreseeing the future and knowing exactly the antagonistic effect of somebody's life through the amounts which can be identified with this person. With the help of numerology estimation, the numerologists usually make individuals mindful in their dreadful time or lucky amounts in order that they can lead their own life indicated by this prediction.

There are tons of methods to acquire completely free numerology suggestions by these pros. Whatever the instance, perhaps not each of those are trustworthy clearly. After all you ought to be considered a bit cautious before carrying this assistance.

Can It Be True to say they are Truly great?

Each aid That's available for nothing is not inferior. Despite the undeniable fact we possess a prognosis for this, nevertheless it is not intelligent. You will find administrations which can be found for just nothing yet perhaps not poor within their own traits plus you are able to confide included. Absolutely free numerology is just one such clinic which is not "poor" in its real sense. Whatever the situation, you will find yet it is not all one of those numerologists that offer free assistance endeavor to loot most the moment. There are skilled numerologists who could possibly offer numerology imagining for nothing.

Where-to See Them?

From the Span of this net nothing is hard to be detected. There are tons of internet numerology centers at which you can find proficient numerologists. They provide you free numerology readings whereby you may acquire mindful about the fate of one's own life; you are able to cause to organize with this too.

Points of Interest of Free Numerology Readings:

The Principle benefit is that you never need to cover this government. On the off likelihood that you are profiting this government because rather than tremendously secure with the accuracy of this practice, you could attempt the free numerology perusing. You can scan web for this form of management and decide on a fair site from where you are able to acquire numerology computation for just nothing.

The Next thing which can attract you such assistance would be it is for the most part done via programmed numerology minicomputers and passed to you. Therefore, there is not any opportunity to get to becoming semi or one sided by you personally and disclose you something amiss. You are certain to acquire 100% exceptional results out of those free numerological readings.

No matter of whether it is liberated numerology or perhaps a compensated aid, you should port with the suitable individual or site who is able to suggest you that the suitable arrangement. Since the matter is excessively touchy plus it can change if you are able to remember that you should be mindful before picking out the numerologist. Numerology imagining is not something tremendously straightforward, it asks tons of fixation, devotion, and study. The pristine estimation of mathematics is demanded here; only a tiny slipup may bring very surprising prediction which finally drives your own life to an exceptional posture.

Organizing Crucial Event in Your Life Through Nemerology

Everything Proven to person using an energy vibration -- and amounts are the exact same. At Numerology, each number (and correspondence) has its own exclusive vibration which comes with an effect upon a mind-blowing account. This manner, numerology may be your analysis of this relationship that letters and numbers come together with your personality and life occasions. It is an antiquated Supernatural science which uncovers the overview of each person's life also it really is but one of the exactly accurate and unbelievable self-improvement apparatuses accessible now.

From the Deep perspective, you will include a soul inside your system that is chose to attest into this lifetime essentially to grow throughout the educational experiences it experiences whether it is here. During the length of the life you will find explicit parts of development your soul has opted to genius and explicit open doors it may possibly desire to tap its voyage. Therefore, as to achieve so you will find explicit personality traits and life requirements it takes to perform its purpose -- the subtleties which can be present on your "amounts"

Since It Were, your numerology profile shows the outline of exactly what your own soul has pre-decided to accomplish this lifetime. Some of the benefits of numerology is it may show your pre-determination and life reason and also the presence exercises you're look end path, that will be significant data on the off likelihood which you want to benefit just as far as you possibly can from the experience.

Numerology Is way beyond foreseeing the near future, or picking the ideal accomplice date, or name. It is the the scaffold between that which you are currently and that you could possibly be. It is really a moving rock which empowers one to continue together with your absolute best life and function as may be likely be.

The Benefits of numerology

The Ideal Advantage of numerology may be your endowment of comprehension. To be warned will be to be forearmed, and numerology provides the direct to an own life therefore you have got a notion of where you are moving and what is instore enrooted. At case you opted to choose a trip to a different goal, wouldn't you wish to advise an idea to find where you are likely to inspect the driving terms before you flourished? Numerology is a tool that could help you with finding your goal also to property there safely, too.

What is More, numerology shows your potential and provides you with what you can reach. It assists with aim setting and organizing your own prospective plus it provides you with consolation you are on the right way. Still another favorite position is the fact that it empowers one to receive all set for potential barriers also to find a deal about doors coming your leadership.

Just in what Manner would numerology manage to boost your own lifetime

Numerology gives your life meaning. It prevents it from having an "intermittent event" to a pre-arranged overview of potential and chance. It gives posture and added knowledge into what is round the bend, also it shows your own pre-determination and lifestyle reasons. It likewise provides an even deeper understanding of your own overall surroundings. In what capacity may not to boost your own life?

Guidelines to Use Numerology

Along Side Any sort of prediction or divination, numerology is better utilized as a guide to supplement your own life. Combined with instinct, trendy led basic direction, and common existence of mind, it needs to be effectively used as a tool to aid you with browsing your life simpler.

Only in the big occasion you were thinking... numerology cannot anticipate winning lottery numbers or even a person's season of passing. (Be as it might, it might be suitable on the off likelihood it may).

CHAPTER FOUR

UNDERSTANDING PERSONAL YEAR

The Personal Year is beneficial in analyzing the pattern of this forthcoming calendar year. To get a Portion of advice regarding what lies ahead at the coming year, calculate your year using this recipe:

From the First location, lessen the day and month of one's debut into the Earth, your birthday, into a lone Dig it. Utilizing my birthday for example, February eighth, this lone digit could be (2+8=10; 1+0=1). At case, your day and month out concerns 11 or 22, the professional amounts, in this event, diminish the quantity to 4 and 2, separately.

Next, Decrease the entire season for that you are earning the computation into your lone Dig it. The calendar year 2015 will secure 8.

Currently, Include the only digit talking into an own birthday into this sole digit speaking into this entire year being known to. This manner, 2015 is a-9-man year for me personally.

The Private year-round plots that the routine of events for the Entire entire year

A Perusing for each near to dwelling year:

Inch
Two
3
4
5
6
7

Individual Year One

A Fresh Beginning on Your Daily Life

The Present season may be the beginning of yet another multi-year bicycle for you personally. It holds the assurance of as an energizing new adventure, together with lifetime carrying on fresh difficulties which produce prepared for the subsequent cycle of 2 years through the duration of your lifetime. This is the chance to spell out your objectives also it is a chance to follow them up. Difficult work may be crucial to find the next job moving. Your physical caliber will probably undoubtedly be upward in this calendar year, maybe greater than it was around for quite some time since you have any exceptional requirements with this extra energy. At the case you cannot or reluctant to respond to the telephone to improve and also create the movement on your entire life the sounds crucial today, your chances may possibly be postponed until the subsequent cycle starts in two decades. Together these lines, you truly feel to be an adventure, a considerable shift in your own life, something fresh. New objectives should be demonstrably set and proceeded from direction of, since it is in fact a fresh beginning of a multiyear cycle also it is better never to select never to proceed ahead now. This is going to undoubtedly be genuinely simple that you complete considering how most of those difficulties and disillusionments of days gone by will generally disappear, leaving the path available for all these brand-new difficulties. This really is an unbelievable moment; utilize it to enhance its full possible benefit.

Individual Year Two

Progress, Cooperation, and tripping

That really is a Number 2-person calendar year. A single year 2 is really a cautious time; annually after you may wind up out of sight and notably in a period of advancement. This really is not the opportunity to induce the problem and try to push beforehand. It is a time for involvement and construction links which may benefit you afterwards; per year for Indices and collecting. Forcefulness may cause problems today. You ought to be create for delays, alternate paths, stoppages, and you also ought to show restraint. This is really a time of little devotion, of assisting, and subtleties must be managed whenever they develop. You will give time and effort to aid another's work. This season may be an evaluation to a poise and enthusiastic sensitivities. This is the chance to increase your abilities to work together at a profitable fashion and this is sometimes trying for you personally around the off likelihood you have essentially worked before. Fight the impulse to panic, trendy, as well as lovely. You will encounter an even of anxious strain in this time; the multi-level takes a propensity to enthused bounds including gloom. Very deep associations by having a single of their contrary gender (counting marriage) may possibly be able to take place throughout a multi calendar year. Whenever married, there is well-suited to become an indication of atmosphere from the relationship throughout a multipurpose calendar year.

Individual Year 3

Social Expansion and ingenious victories

That really is a No 3 year. This is a societal, cheerful calendar year, also it often will generally ooze brilliant and joyful vibrations. This is just a year after which you will have to ascertain the status of older companies and expand your band of friends to include several fresh ones. Sentiment and relationships can blossom. You are slanted to call home to its fullest currently, irrespective of whether you want to pay for dearly in the future. You are most likely going to be amiable and the tap of responsibility will probably seem to get published a bit of a You're slanted to distribute your energies and attempt an inordinate quantity of things simultaneously. You can safely have a rest to really have a chunk yet combat the compulsion to completely return to generating some wonderful memories; remember your own objectives. A-3 individual year can be an adequate period to cultivate individual advanced abilities, notably those diagnosed using expressions of the individual encounter and verbal aptitudes. Acknowledgment such manner is probable this past year.

Even though This is sometimes a joyous year to the scope human articulation and exercises have been all concerned, it may be described as a deplorable year on the industry scene. Some for its most part moot mindset in that state can cause poor decisions and unrealistic, unfinished plans. This is not likely going to become a superb season for the own funds, and it is blessed that the subsequent year is designed to refund these effects.

Individual Year 4

Difficult Slow and work, nevertheless persistent advancement

That really is a Number 4-person year for you. The prior year silliness will now be overlooked, whilst the inevitable problems facing everybody else are explained. Here is an occasion of work and effort if you must hunker down to the job that has to be carried out. An occasion of delving in and hoeing, a recovery of discretion. From various points of perspective, be as it might, it is a tough calendar year, when significant effort succeeds to deliver outcomes that are spectacular. 1-point forwards and 2 rear may possibly be seemingly the case more frequently than not. This is really a hierarchical time and you also ought to consider a gander in your current and beyond demonstration within an excessively hard lighting. It is a chance to acquire sorted out and then bring yourself fair. Obligations will increment, amplifying the effort and difficult work anticipated to maintain a moderate amount of life. Well-being and dietary plan should be examined for this year because physical obstacle is low, and you also may possibly prove to be vulnerable to diseases. A clean-up of problems is now all together since you should prepare yourself for quite a tumultuous season beforehand.

Individual Year 5

Feeling Complimentary and Totally Free

That really is a Number multi-level, a period of significant change on your daily life. Skylines are development and extended is much less obstructed. You are most likely going to produce various new companies that this season since societal drills are extended. This is just a year that is brought/will attract energy and experience and more opportunity when you have struck by late. This is really a time for feeling liberated and liberated; for moving from older programs in a helpful method. On the off likelihood that you have shrouded through this former calendar year, at this time is the perfect chance to seek out fresh headings.

The Situation With just one year 5 is now your tendency to exude energies every which way. The power to complete detail work would be constrained today plus it is likely to force you to feel bound. Overall, this type of freewheeling year that is bound to take substantial modifications to your own life, your own vocation, your own family condition, your residence.

Individual Year 6

Love, Family, Home and Responsibility

That is a No 6 Personal Year for you. A single year 6 will generally reevaluate expanding duties and a growing stress for family members, friends and family, and beloved companions. It may be described as a year when you are approached to create several changes all through your lifetime, or penances for people on your family or close friend system. This really is not normally every year for significant accomplishments, but instead a chance to bargain with those improvements in accord with your structures which may be required or essential, and for completing ventures started. Tries will seem to proceed therefore slowly regularly. You should expect to get a generally amazing year as much as family, home, and Profession problems are all concerned. Your ardent commerce with the people that are close you should be in its absolute best throughout this calendar year. The most substantial issue is usually to be more excited to admit that a slower pace and be sure to comprehend the stability and agreement that the average person season number 6 will attract.

Individual Year 7

A span for comprehension and investigation

A-7 Individual year promises to be quite a thoughtful calendar year, an occasion of a few disturbance and reflection between very energetic years through the duration of your lifetime. This season should supply you with sometime for improving a few understandings on your own, and you are well-suited to commit an adequate object of energy in examination. It will soon be good for one to commit energy or at exercises that are calm, as free of outside assignments as can possibly be enabled. You ought to try to flee from pressures. This is an adequate season to contemplate the past and look for what is in the future. This will not generally be an occasion of activity, but instead an occasion of tripping along with advancement. Probably one of the very productive exercises in having to draw for one year 7 is a lot of study and writing, for the capability to believe clearly, research, and incorporate that your musings is crested as of this time. Your skill for comprehension and research is in its absolute best. It would not be odd that you have a look of coolness and break throughout a multipurpose calendar year. Absolutely, it is most effective for one really to concentrate in your own presents and your aptitudes by having a conclusion goal to use the period you must enhance them. Maybe you can find a chance to obtain training or invest completely free energy things being equal and contemplation.

Individual Year 8

Achievement And funding developments

That really is a Number 8-person year for you. That really is the skill, a time when you can create significant walks into your life. Anyhow after a medium and reflective span (just one season 7), you can start setting a couple stirrings of ambitions. Here is a period of critical decisions and significant accomplishments. Movement can be the keynote today, and you are certain to end up specially involved and included. Open doors to get headway and recognition for past and present work is likely planning to come to fruition in this season. You might have things moving to you since you tap and behave. It is simple that you buff out and develop into an orderly way. On the off likelihood that you are in all slanted, that can be merely a chance to exude certainty and ability, as the others may generally be amenable to a control and administration. Your skill and status potential are at a pinnacle of those two years human epicycle that shuts toward the final of the subsequent calendar year.

Individual Year 9

Reflection and Reaching Out

That really is a 9-man year for you. That really is a period of consummations, completing, also if You're well-suited to take stock of those several elements all through your Life, a number which you might be no doubt thankful for, and also many others you may possibly Need to modify. You are Likely to explore Aged attributes, beliefs, And the ideas you just thought were significant. This should be the stage of that you then become associated with others and committing could turn Outside to be increasingly important that just paying special mind on your own. You will likewise Acquire mindful of a lure to collective together with character, as idealist Wants turn into a whole lot more relaxed than formerly. A Lot of items You Have Been doing work for if arrived at consummation in this calendar year, and you may in General get ready for conflict to get the beginning of yet another multi season cycle.

CPSIA information can be obtained
at www.ICGtesting.com
Printed in the USA
LVHW050930010621
689024LV00004B/246